STUART

# The ESSENTIALS® of
REGISTERED TRADEMARK

# UNITED STATES HISTORY

## — 1500 to 1789 —
## From Colony to Republic

**Steven E. Woodworth, Ph.D.**
Assistant Professor of History
Toccoa Falls College
Toccoa, Georgia

D0191099

*Research & Education Association*
61 Ethel Road West
Piscataway, New Jersey 08854

THE ESSENTIALS ®
OF UNITED STATES HISTORY
1500 to 1789
From Colony to Republic

1998 PRINTING

Copyright © 1996, 1990 by Research & Education
Association. All rights reserved. No part of this
book may be reproduced in any form without
permission of the publisher.

Printed in the United States of America

Library of Congress Catalog Card Number 96-67268

International Standard Book Number 0-87891-712-8

ESSENTIALS is a registered trademark of
Research & Education Association, Piscataway, New Jersey 08854

# What the "Essentials of History" Will Do for You

REA's "Essentials of History" series offers a new approach to the study of history that is different from what has been available previously. Each book in the series has been designed to steer a sensible middle course, by including neither too much nor too little information.

Compared with conventional history outlines, the "Essentials of History" offer far more detail, with fuller explanations and interpretations of historical events and developments. Compared with voluminous historical tomes and textbooks, the "Essentials of History" offer a far more concise, less ponderous overview of each of the periods they cover.

The "Essentials of History" are intended primarily to aid students in studying history, doing homework, writing papers and preparing for exams. The books are organized to provide quick access to information and explanations of the important events, dates, and persons of the period. The books can be used in conjunction with any text. They will save hours of study and preparation time while providing a firm grasp and insightful understanding of the subject matter.

Instructors too will find the "Essentials of History" useful. The books can assist in reviewing or modifying course outlines. They also can assist with preparation of exams, as well as serve as an efficient memory refresher.

In sum, the "Essentials of History" will prove to be handy reference sources at all times.

The authors of the series are respected experts in their fields. They present clear, well-reasoned explanations and interpretations of the complex political, social, cultural, economic and philosophical issues and developments which characterize each era.

In preparing these books REA has made every effort to assure their accuracy and maximum usefulness. We are confident that each book will prove enjoyable and valuable to its user.

Dr. Max Fogiel, Program Director

## *About the Author*

Steven E. Woodworth received the Rice Presidential Recognition Award in 1983, a scholarship from the University of Hamburg German Academic Exchange Service in 1982-1983, and a Rice University Graduate Fellowship from 1983 to 1987. His professional memberships include the American Historical Association, the Southern Historical Association, and the Conference on Faith and History. His special expertise includes the Civil War and Reconstruction era, the U.S. Constitution and legal history, U.S. military history, and U.S. colonial and revolutionary history. He is the author of *Jefferson Davis and His Generals: The Failure of Confederate Command in the West.*

Dr. Woodworth is currently an assistant professor of History at Toccoa Falls College in Toccoa, Georgia. He was previously an instructor at Bartlesville Wesleyan College in Bartlesville, Oklahoma.

# CONTENTS

# CHAPTER 1

# THE AGE OF EXPLORATION

## 1.1   THE TREATY OF TORDESILLAS

Though Columbus denied to his dying day having discovered a continent previously unknown to Europeans, geographers thought otherwise and named the new lands after Amerigo Vespucci, an Italian member of a Portuguese expedition to South America whose widely reprinted report suggested a new world had been found.

Excited by the gold Columbus had brought back from America, Ferdinand and Isabella, joint monarchs of Spain, sought formal confirmation of their ownership of these new lands. They feared the interference of Portugal, which was at that time a powerful seafaring nation and had been active in overseas exploration. At Spain's urging the pope drew a "Line of Demarcation" one hundred leagues west of the Cape Verde Islands, dividing the heathen world into two equal parts – that east of the line for Portugal and that west of it for Spain.

Because this line tended to be unduly favorable to Spain, and because Portugal had the stronger navy, the two countries worked out the Treaty of Tordesillas (1493), by which the line was moved farther west. As a result, Brazil eventually became a Portuguese colony, while Spain maintained claims to the rest of the Americas. As other European nations joined the hunt for colonies, they tended to ignore the Treaty of Tordesillas.

## 1.2 THE SPANISH CONQUISTADORES

To conquer the Americas the Spanish monarchs used their powerful army, led by independent Spanish adventurers known as conquistadores, who sought to win glory and wealth and spread the Roman Catholic faith, and "were not squeamish about the means they used" to do so.

At first the conquistadores confined their attentions to the Caribbean islands, where the European diseases they unwittingly carried with them devastated the local Indian populations, who had no immunities against such diseases.

After about 1510 the conquistadores turned their attention to the American mainland. In 1513 Vasco Nunez de Balboa crossed the isthmus of Panama and became the first European to see the Pacific Ocean, which he claimed for Spain. The same year Juan Ponce de Leon explored Florida in search of gold and a fabled fountain of youth. He found neither but claimed Florida for Spain.

In 1519 Hernando (Hernan) Cortes led his dramatic expedition against the Aztecs of Mexico. Aided by the fact that the Indians at first mistook him for god, as well as by firearms, armor, horses, and (unknown to him) smallpox germs, all previously unknown in America, Cortes destroyed the Aztec empire and won enormous riches.

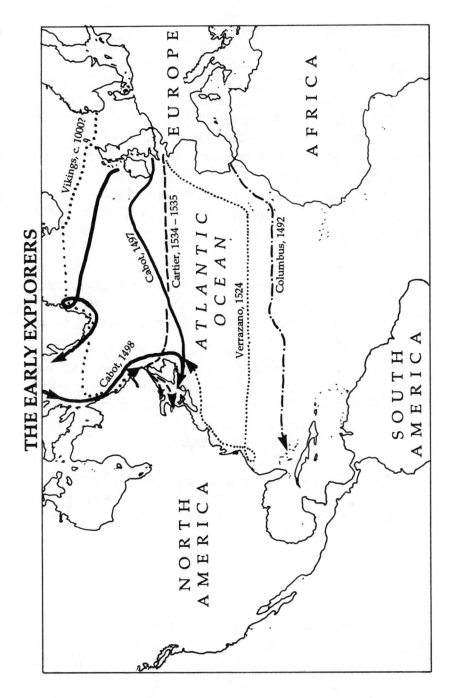

THE EARLY EXPLORERS

EUROPE

AFRICA

Vikings, c. 1000?

Cabot, 1497

Cartier, 1534 – 1535

ATLANTIC
OCEAN

Verrazano, 1524

Columbus, 1492

Cabot, 1498

NORTH
AMERICA

SOUTH
AMERICA

Other conquistadores endeavored to follow Cortes' example, sometimes with similar results. By the 1550s such fortune seekers had conquered much of South America.

In North America the Spaniards sought in vain for riches. In 1528 Panfilio de Narvaez led a disastrous expedition through the Gulf Coast region from which only four of the original four hundred men returned. One of them, Cabeza de Vaca, brought with him a story of seven great cities full of gold (the "Seven Cities of Cibola") somewhere to the north. In response to this, two Spanish expeditions explored the interior of North America:

1) Hernando de Soto led a six hundred-man expedition (1539 – 1541) through what is now the southeastern United States, penetrating as far west as Oklahoma and discovering the Mississippi River, on whose banks de Soto was buried.

2) Francisco Vasquez de Coronado led an expedition (1540 – 1542) from Mexico, north across the Rio Grande and through New Mexico, Arizona, Texas, Oklahoma, and Kansas. Some of Coronado's men were the first Europeans to see the Grand Canyon.

While neither expedition discovered rich Indian civilizations to plunder, both increased Europe's knowledge of the interior of North America and asserted Spain's territorial claims to the continent.

## 1.3   NEW SPAIN

Spain administered its new holdings as an autocratic, rigidly controlled empire in which everything was to benefit the parent country. Tight control of even mundane matters was

# THE CONQUISTADORES

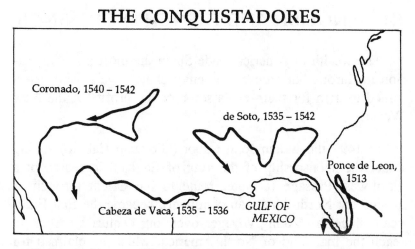

carried out by a suffocating bureaucracy run directly from Madrid. Annual treasure fleets carried the riches of the New World to Spain for the furtherance of its military-political goals in Europe.

As population pressures were low in sixteenth-century Spain, only about 200,000 Spaniards came to America during that time. To deal with the consequent labor shortages and as a reward to successful conquistadores the Spaniards developed a system of large manors or estates (*encomiendas*) with Indian slaves ruthlessly managed for the benefit of the conquistadores. The *encomienda* system was later replaced by the similar but somewhat milder *hacienda* system. As the Indian population died from overwork and European diseases, Spaniards began importing African slaves to supply their labor needs. Society in New Spain was rigidly stratified, with the highest level reserved for natives of Spain (*peninsulares*) and the next for those of Spanish parentage born in the New World (*creoles*). Those of mixed or Indian blood occupied lower levels.

After 1535 New Spain was ruled by a viceroy, a Spanish nobleman appointed by the king to act as his representative in the colonies.

## 1.4   ENGLISH AND FRENCH BEGINNINGS

The wealth of America made Spain the most powerful nation in Europe but aroused the envy of her rivals, who determined to gain for themselves some of the profits of the New World.

In 1497 the Italian John Cabot (Giovanni Caboto) sailing under the sponsorship of the king of England in search of a Northwest Passage (a water route to the Orient through or around the North American continent), became the first European, since the Viking voyages over four centuries earlier, to reach the mainland of North America, which he claimed for England.

In 1524 the king of France authorized another Italian, Giovannia da Verrazzano, to undertake a mission similar to Cabot's. Endeavoring to duplicate the achievement of Spaniard Ferdinand Magellan, who had five years earlier found a way around the southern tip of South America, Verrazzano followed the American coast from present-day North Carolina to Maine.

Beginning in 1534, Jacques Cartier, also authorized by the king of France, mounted three expeditions to the area of the St. Lawrence River, which he believed might be the hoped-for Northwest Passage. He explored up the river as far as the site of Montreal, where rapids prevented him, as he thought, from continuing to China. He claimed the area for France before abandoning his last expedition and returning to France in 1542. France made no further attempts to explore or colonize in America for sixty-five years.

England showed little interest in America as well during most of the sixteenth century. This delay had two important consequences:

1) When the English finally did begin colonization, commercial capitalism in England had advanced to the point that the English efforts were supported by private rather than government funds, allowing the English colonists to enjoy a greater degree of freedom from government interference.

2) The Protestant Reformation had taken place and England, a Protestant nation, was involved in a bitter struggle with the supporters of Roman Catholicism.

## 1.5  SIXTEENTH-CENTURY EUROPE

The Protestant Reformation itself, along with the turmoil it brought, was one of the reasons that England and France gave little attention to America during the sixteenth century. Both countries had problems enough at home.

The Reformation began in Germany in 1517 under the leadership of Martin Luther. Luther believed that many practices of Roman Catholicism were contrary to the teachings of the Bible. Particularly, he believed and taught that salvation was by faith alone, rather than by Catholicism's elaborate system of sacraments.

The Reformation spread to England as a result of dynastic politics. King Henry VIII broke with Rome in order to divorce his first wife, marry a second, and, he hoped, obtain a male heir to secure his dynasty's succession. Aside from breaking with the pope – who had refused to grant his request for a divorce – Henry wanted to retain most of the trappings of Catholicism, but the Reformation could not be contained. In 1539 William Tyndale and Miles Coverdale brought out an English translation of the Bible, causing many to feel Henry's reformation had not gone far enough.

The son Henry finally got to succeed him embraced a more complete Protestantism but died after six years on the throne, only to be succeeded by his sister (Henry's daughter), Mary. Mary endeavored to reconvert England to Catholicism by burning Protestants at the stake. Many prominent English Protestants fled to Geneva, Switzerland, where they were influenced by the thinking of John Calvin.

Calvin stressed the sovereignty of God and the helplessness of man, and taught the doctrine of predestination, according to which God elected in advance which persons would be saved and which damned. Though in Calvin's scheme hard work and righteous living would not get one into heaven, they might be a sign of God's election; and therefore Calvin's followers searched their lives constantly for such manifestations. Calvin's thinking had an enormous influence on British Protestantism and, through it, early American thought and society.

Upon the death of Mary in 1558 the exiled Protestant leaders returned to England and soon gained a large following. They began to be called Puritans, for their desire to purify the incompletely reformed Church of England.

Partially as a result of the New World rivalries and partially through differences between Protestants and Catholic countries, the sixteenth century was a violent time both in Europe and in America. French Protestants, called Hugenots, who attempted to escape persecution in Catholic France by settling in the New World were massacred by the Spaniards. One such incident led the Spaniards, nervous about any possible encroachment on what they considered to be their exclusive holdings in America, to build a fort that became the beginning of a settlement at St. Augustine, Florida, the oldest city in North America. Spanish priests ventured north from St. Augustine, but no permanent settlements were built in the interior.

French and especially English sea captains made great sport of and considerable profit from the plundering the Spaniards of the wealth they had first plundered from the Indians. One of the most successful English captains, Francis Drake, sailed around South America and raided the Spanish settlements on the Pacific coast of Central America before continuing on to California, which he claimed for England and named Nova Albion. Drake then returned to England by sailing around the world. England's Queen Elizabeth, sister and Protestant successor to Mary, had been quietly investing in Drake's highly profitable voyages. On Drake's return from his round-the-world voyage, Elizabeth openly showed her approval.

Angered by this as well as by Elizabeth's support of the Protestant cause in Europe, Spain's King Philip II in 1588 dispatched a mighty fleet, the Spanish Armada, to conquer England. Instead, the Armada was defeated by the English navy and largely destroyed by storms in the North Sea. This victory established England as a great power and moved it a step closer to overseas colonization, although the war with Spain continued until 1604.

## 1.6   GILBERT, RALEIGH, AND THE FIRST ENGLISH ATTEMPTS

English nobleman Sir Humphrey Gilbert believed England should found colonies and find a Northwest Passage. In 1576 he sent English sea captain Martin Frobisher to look for such a passage. Frobisher scouted along the inhospitable northeastern coast of Canada and brought back large amounts of a yellow metal that turned out to be fool's gold. In 1578 Gilbert obtained a charter allowing him to found a colony with his own funds and guaranteeing the prospective colonists all the rights of those born and residing in England, thus setting an important precedent for future colonial charters. His attempts to found a colony in Newfoundland failed, and while pursuing these endeavors he was lost at sea.

With the queen's permission, Gilbert's work was taken up by his half-brother, Sir Walter Raleigh. Raleigh turned his attention to a more southerly portion of the North American coastline, which he named Virginia, in honor of England's unmarried queen. He selected as a site for the first settlement Roanoke Island just off the coast of present-day North Carolina.

After one abortive attempt, a group of 114 settlers – men, women, and children – were landed in July 1587. Shortly thereafter, Virginia Dare became the first English child born in America. Later that year the expedition's leader, John White, returned to England to secure additional supplies. Delayed by the war with Spain he did not return until 1590, when he found the colony deserted. It is not known what became of the Roanoke settlers.

After this failure, Raleigh was forced by financial constraints to abandon his attempts to colonize Virginia. Hampered by unrealistic expectations, inadequate financial resources, and the ongoing war with Spain, English interest in American colonization was submerged for fifteen years.

# CHAPTER 2

# THE BEGINNINGS OF COLONIZATION

## 2.1 VIRGINIA

In the first decade of the 1600s, Englishmen, exhilarated by the recent victory over Spain and influenced by the writings of Richard Hakluyt (who urged American colonization as the way to national greatness and the spread of the gospel), once again undertook to plant colonies.

Two groups of merchants gained charters from Queen Elizabeth's successor, James I. One group of merchants was based in London and received a charter to North America between what are now the Hudson and the Cape Fear Rivers. The other was based in Plymouth and was granted the right to colonize in North America from the Potomac to the northern border of present-day Maine. They were called the Virginia Company of London and the Virginia Company of Plymouth, respectively.

These were joint-stock companies, which raised their capital by the sale of shares of stock. Companies of this sort had already been used to finance and carry on English trade with Russia, Africa, and the Middle East.

The Plymouth Company, in 1607, attempted to plant a colony in Maine, but after one winter the colonists became discouraged and returned to Britain. Thereafter the Plymouth Company folded.

The Virginia Company of London, in 1607, sent out an expedition of three ships with 104 men to plant a colony some forty miles up the James River from Chesapeake Bay. Like the river on which it was located, the new settlement was named Jamestown in honor of England's king. It became the first permanent English settlement in North America, but for a time it appeared to be going the way of the earlier attempts.

During the early years of Jamestown, the majority of the settlers died of starvation, various diseases, or hostile action by Indians. Though the losses were continuously replaced by new settlers, the colony's survival remained in doubt for a number of years. There were several reasons for these difficulties:

1) The entire colony was owned by the company, and all members shared the profits regardless of how much or how little they worked. There was thus a lack of incentive.

2) Many of the settlers were gentlemen, who considered themselves too good to work at growing the food the colony needed to survive. Others were simply unambitious and little inclined to work in any case.

3) The settlers had come with the expectation of finding

gold or other quick and easy riches and wasted much time looking for these while they should have been providing for their survival.

4) For purposes of defense, the settlement had been sited on a peninsula formed by a bend in the river; but this low and swampy location proved to be a breeding ground for all sorts of diseases and, at high tide, even contaminated the settlers' drinking supply with sea water.

5) Relations with Powhatan, the powerful local Indian chief, were at best uncertain and often openly hostile, with disastrous results for the colonists.

In 1608 and 1609 the dynamic and ruthless leadership of John Smith kept the colony from collapsing. Smith's rule was, "He who works not, eats not." After Smith returned to England in late 1609 the condition of the colony again became critical.

Back in England, the London Company investors refused to give up and continued to send settlers, often without adequate supplies.

In 1612, a Virginia resident named John Rolfe discovered that a superior strain of tobacco, native to the West Indies, could be grown in Virginia. There was a large market for this tobacco in Europe, and Rolfe's discovery gave Virginia a major cash crop.

Tobacco was soon being grown enthusiastically and in large amounts in Virginia, but the colony still had serious problems. Disease and Indian trouble continued to take a fantastic toll of life; and in England, Virginia was earning a well-deserved reputation as a death trap.

To secure more settlers and boost Virginia's shrinking labor force, the company moved to make immigration possible for Britain's poor who were without economic opportunity at home or financial means to procure transportation to America. This was achieved by means of the indenture system, by which a poor worker's passage to America was paid by an American planter (or the company itself), and in exchange, was indentured to work for the planter (or the company) for a specified number of years. The system was open to abuse and often resulted in the mistreatment of the indentured servants.

To control the workers thus shipped to Virginia, as well as the often lazy and unruly colonists already present, the company gave its governors in America dictatorial powers. Governors such as Lord De La Warr, Sir Thomas Gates, and Sir Thomas Dale made use of such powers, imposing a harsh rule.

For such reasons, and its well-known reputation as a death trap, Virginia continued to attract inadequate numbers of immigrants. To solve this, a reform-minded faction within the company proposed a new approach, and under its leader Edwin Sandys made changes designed to attract more settlers.

1) Colonists were promised the same rights they had in England.

2) A representative assembly – the House of Burgesses – was founded in 1619, the first in America.

3) Private ownership of land was instituted.

Despite these reforms, Virginia's unhealthy reputation kept many Englishmen away. Large numbers of indentured servants were brought in, especially young, single men. The first Africans were brought to Virginia in 1619 but were treated as indentured servants rather than slaves.

Virginia's Indian relations remained difficult. In 1622 an Indian massacre took the lives of 347 settlers. In 1644 the Indians struck again, massacring some 300 more. Shortly thereafter, the coastal Indians were subdued and no longer presented a serious threat.

Impressed by the potential profits from tobacco growing, King James I determined to have Virginia for himself. Using the high mortality and the 1622 massacre as a pretext, in 1624 he revoked the London Company's charter and made Virginia a royal colony. This pattern was followed throughout colonial history; both company colonies and proprietary colonies (see 2.7 below) tended eventually to become royal colonies.

Upon taking over Virginia, James revoked all political rights and the representative assembly – he did not believe in such things – but fifteen years later his son, Charles I, was forced, by constant pressure from the Virginians and the continuing need to attract more settlers, to restore these rights.

## 2.2 NEW FRANCE

Shortly after England returned to the business of colonization, France renewed its interest in the areas previously visited by such French explorers as Jacques Cartier.

The French opened with the Indians a lucrative trade in furs, plentiful in America and much sought after in Europe.

The St. Lawrence River was the French gateway to the interior of North America. In 1608 Samuel de Champlain established a trading post in Quebec, from which the rest of what became New France eventually spread.

Relatively small numbers of Frenchmen came to America,

# THE FRENCH IN THE INTERIOR

Champlain,
1608 – 1609

Marquette, 1673

LaSalle, 1681 – 1682

and partially because of this they were generally able to maintain good relations with the Indians. French Canadians were energetic in exploring and claiming new lands for France.

French exploration and settlement spread through the Great Lakes region and the valleys of the Mississippi and Ohio Rivers. In 1673 Jacques Marquette explored the Mississippi Valley, and in 1682 Sieur de la Salle followed the river to its mouth. French settlements in the Midwest were not generally real towns, but rather forts and trading posts serving the fur trade.

Throughout its history, New France was handicapped by an

inadequate population and a lack of support by the parent country.

## 2.3   NEW NETHERLANDS

Other countries also took an interest in North America. In 1609 Holland sent an Englishman named Henry Hudson to explore for them in search of a Northwest Passage. In this endeavor Hudson discovered the river that bears his name.

Arrangements were made to trade with the Iroquois Indians for furs, especially beaver pelts for the hats then popular in Europe. In 1624 Dutch trading outposts were established on Manhattan Island (New Amsterdam) and at the site of present-day Albany (Fort Orange). A profitable fur trade was carried on and became the main source of revenue for the Dutch West India Company, the joint-stock company that ran the colony.

To encourage enough farming to keep the colony supplied with food, the Dutch instituted the *patroon* system, by which large landed estates would be given to wealthy men who transported at least fifty families to New Netherlands. These families would then become tenant farmers on the estate of the patroon who had transported them. As Holland's home economy was healthy, few Dutch felt desperate enough to take up such unattractive terms.

New Netherlands was, in any case, internally weak and unstable. It was poorly governed by inept and lazy governors; and its population was a mixture of people from all over Europe as well as many African slaves, forming what historians have called an "unstable pluralism."

## 2.4  THE PILGRIMS AT PLYMOUTH

Many Englishmen came from England for religious reasons. For the most part, these fell into two groups, Puritans (see 1.5 above) and Separatists. Though similar in many respects to the Puritans, the Separatists believed the Church of England was beyond saving and so felt they must separate from it.

One group of Separatists, suffering government harassment, fled to Holland. Dissatisfied there, they decided to go to America and thus became the famous Pilgrims.

Led by William Bradford, they departed in 1620, having obtained from the London Company a charter to settle just south of the Hudson River. Driven by storms, their ship, the *Mayflower*, made landfall at Cape Cod in Massachusetts; and they decided it was God's will for them to settle in that area. This, however, put them outside the jurisdiction of any established government; and so before going ashore they drew up and signed the Mayflower Compact, establishing a foundation for orderly government based on the consent of the governed.

After a difficult first winter that saw many die, the Pilgrims went on to establish a quiet and modestly prosperous colony. After a number of years of hard work they were able to buy out the investors who had originally financed their voyage and thus gain greater autonomy.

## 2.5  THE MASSACHUSETTS BAY COLONY

The Puritans were far more numerous than the Separatists. Contrary to stereotype, they did not dress in drab clothes and were not ignorant or bigoted. They did, however, take the Bible and their religion seriously and felt the Anglican Church still retained too many unscriptural practices left over from Roman Catholicism.

King James I had no use for the Puritans but refrained from bringing on a confrontation with their growing political power. His son, Charles I, determined in 1629 to persecute the Puritans aggressively and to rule without the Puritan-dominated parliament. This course would lead eventually (ten years later) to civil war, but in the meantime some of the Puritans decided to set up a community in America.

To accomplish their purpose, they sought in 1629 to charter a joint-stock company to be called the Massachusetts Bay Company. Whether because Charles was glad to be rid of the Puritans or because he did not realize the special nature of this joint-stock company, the charter was granted. Further, the charter neglected to specify where the company's headquarters should be located. Taking advantage of this unusual omission, the Puritans determined to make their headquarters in the colony itself, three thousand miles from meddlesome royal officials.

Under the leadership of John Winthrop, who taught that a new colony should provide the whole world a model of what a Christian society ought to be, the Puritans carefully organized their venture and, upon arriving in Massachusetts in 1630, did not undergo the "starving time" that had often plagued other first-year colonies.

The government of Massachusetts developed to include a governor and a representative assembly (called the General Court) selected by the "freemen" – adult male church members. As Massachusetts' population increased (20,000 Puritans had come by 1642 in what came to be called the Great Migration), new towns were chartered, each town being granted a large tract of land by the Massachusetts government. As in European villages, these towns consisted of a number of houses clustered around the church house and the village green. Farmland was located around the outside of the town. In each new town the elect – those who testified of having experienced saving grace – covenanted together as a church.

## 2.6 RHODE ISLAND, CONNECTICUT, AND NEW HAMPSHIRE

Puritans saw their colony not as a place to do whatever might strike one's fancy, but as a place to serve God and build His kingdom. Dissidents would only be tolerated insofar as they did not interfere with the colony's mission. Dissidents banished from Massachusetts, or those who while in general agreement felt they might be more comfortable elsewhere, founded several other colonies.

One such dissident was Roger Williams. A Puritan preacher, Williams was received warmly in Massachusetts in 1631; but he had a talent for carrying things to their logical (or sometimes not so logical) extreme, and though he tried one town after another he could never find a church that was pure enough for him. Each imagined impurity he denounced in extreme terms. When his activities became disruptive he was asked to leave the colony.

To avoid having to return to England – where he would have been even less welcome – he fled to the wilderness around Narragansett Bay, bought land from the Indians, and founded the settlement of Providence (1636), soon populated by his many followers.

Another dissident was Anne Hutchinson, who openly

taught things contrary to Puritan doctrine – that there was no need to obey the law of God, that a godly life was no indication that one was among the elect, and that a large number of leading Puritan ministers in Massachusetts were unconverted, among other things. Called before the General Court to answer for her teachings, she claimed to have had special revelations from God superseding the Bible. This was unthinkable in Puritan theology and led to Hutchinson's banishment from the colony. She also migrated to the area around Narragansett Bay and with her followers founded Portsmouth (1638). She later migrated still farther west and was killed by Indians.

In 1644 Roger Williams secured from Parliament a charter combining Providence, Portsmouth, and other settlements that had sprung up in the area into the colony of Rhode Island. Through Williams' influence the colony granted complete religious toleration.

Rhode Island tended to be populated by such exiles and troublemakers as could not find welcome in the other colonies or in Europe. It suffered constant political turmoil.

Connecticut was founded by Puritans who had slight religious disagreements with the leadership of Massachusetts. In 1636 Thomas Hooker led a group of settlers westward to found Hartford. Hooker, though a good friend of Massachusetts Governor John Winthrop, felt he was exercising somewhat more authority than was good. Others also moved into Connecticut from Massachusetts. In 1639 the Fundamental Orders of Connecticut, the first written constitution in America, were drawn up, providing for representative government.

In 1637 a group of Puritans led by John Davenport founded the neighboring colony of New Haven. Davenport and his followers felt that Winthrop, far from being too strict, was not

# THE NEW ENGLAND COLONIES

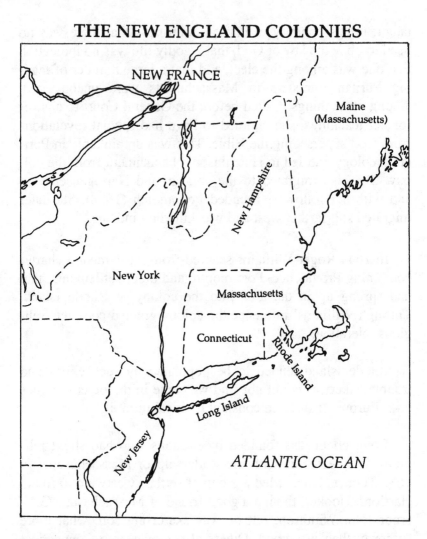

being strict enough.

In 1662 a new charter combined both New Haven and Connecticut into an officially recognized colony of Connecticut.

New Hampshire's settlement did not involve any disagreement at all among the Puritans. It was simply settled as an overflow from Massachusetts. In 1677 King Charles II chartered the separate royal colony of New Hampshire. It remained economically dependent on Massachusetts.

## 2.7  MARYLAND

By the 1630s, the English crown was taking a more direct interest in exercising control over the colonies, and therefore turned away from the practice of granting charters to joint-stock companies, and towards granting such charters to single individuals or groups of individuals known as proprietors.

The proprietors would actually own the colony, and would be directly responsible for it to the king, in an arrangement similar to the feudalism of medieval Europe. Though this was seen as providing more opportunity for royal control and less for autonomy on the part of the colonists, in practice proprietary colonies turned out much like the company colonies because settlers insisted on self-government.

The first proprietary colony was Maryland, granted in 1632 to George Calvert, Lord Baltimore. It was to be located just north of the Potomac River and to be at the same time a reward for Calvert's loyal service to the king as well as a refuge for English Catholics, of which Calvert was one. George Calvert died before the colony could be planted, but the venture was carried forward by his son Cecilius.

From the start more Protestants than Catholics came. To protect the Catholic minority Calvert approved an Act of Religious Toleration (1649) guaranteeing political rights to Christians of all persuasions. Calvert also allowed a representative assembly.

Economically and socially Maryland developed as a virtual carbon copy of neighboring Virginia.

# THE SOUTHERN COLONIES

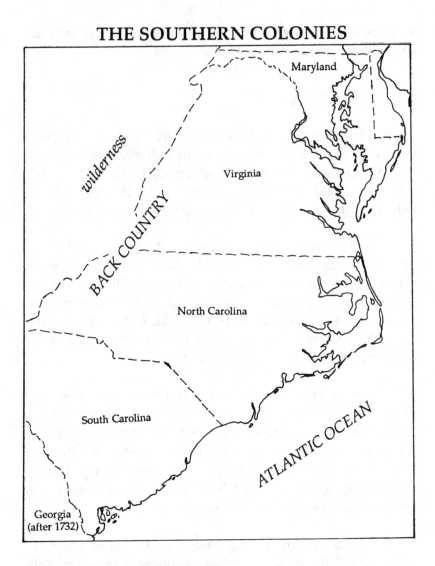

## 2.8   THE CAROLINAS

In 1663 Charles II, having recently been restored to the throne after a twenty-year Puritan revolution that had seen his father beheaded, moved to reward eight of the noblemen who had helped him regain the crown by granting them a charter for all the lands lying south of Virginia and north of Spanish Florida.

The new colony was called Carolina, after the king. In hopes of attracting settlers, the proprietors came up with an elaborate plan for a hierarchical, almost feudal, society. Not surprisingly this proved unworkable, and despite offers of generous land grants to settlers, the Carolinas grew slowly.

The area of North Carolina developed as an overflow from Virginia with similar economic and cultural features. South Carolina was settled by English planters from the island of Barbados, who founded Charles Town (Charleston) in 1670. These planters brought with them their black slaves; and thus, unlike the Chesapeake colonies of Virginia and Maryland, South Carolina had slavery as a fully developed institution from the outset. South Carolina eventually found rice to be a profitable staple crop.

## 2.9   NEW YORK AND NEW JERSEY

Charles II, though immoral and dissolute, was cunning and had an eye for increasing Britain's power. The Dutch colony of New Netherlands, lying between the Chesapeake and the New England colonies, caught his eye as a likely target for British expansion.

In 1664 Charles gave his brother, James, Duke of York, title to all the Dutch lands in America, provided James conquered them first. To do this James sent an invasion fleet under the command of Colonel Richard Nicols. New Amsterdam fell almost without a shot and became New York.

James was adamantly opposed to representative assemblies and ordered that there should be none in New York. To avoid

# THE MIDDLE COLONIES

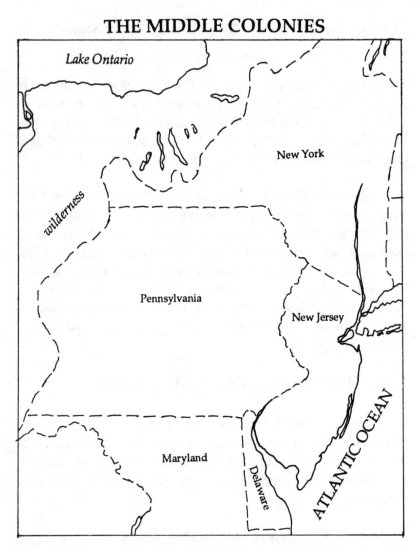

Lake Ontario

wilderness

New York

Pennsylvania

New Jersey

Maryland

Delaware

ATLANTIC OCEAN

unrest Nicols shrewdly granted as many other civil and political rights as possible; but residents, particularly Puritans who had settled on Long Island, continued to agitate for self-government. Finally in the 1680s James relented, only to break his promise when he became king in 1685.

To add to the confusion in the newly renamed colony,

James granted a part of his newly acquired domain to John Lord Berkeley and Sir George Carteret (two of the Carolina proprietors) who named their new proprietorship New Jersey. James neglected to tell Colonel Nicols of this, with the result that both Nicols, on the one hand, and Carteret and Berkeley, on the other, were granting title to the same land – to different settlers. Conflicting claims of land ownership plagued New Jersey for decades, being used by the crown in 1702 as a pretext to take over New Jersey as a royal colony.

# CHAPTER 3

# THE COLONIAL WORLD

## 3.1 LIFE IN THE COLONIES

Seventeenth-century New England grew not only from immigration but also from natural increase. The typical New England family had more children than the typical English or Chesapeake family, and more of those children survived to have families of their own. A New Englander could expect to live 15 to 20 years longer than his counterpart in the parent country and 25 to 30 years longer than his fellow colonist in the Chesapeake.

Because of the continuity provided by these longer life-spans, because the Puritans had migrated as intact family units, and because of the homogeneous nature of the Puritan New England colonies, New England enjoyed a much more stable and well-ordered society than did the Chesapeake colonies.

Puritans placed great importance on the family, which in their society was highly patriarchal. Young people were generally subject to their parents' direction in the matter of when and whom they would marry. Few defied this system, and illegitimate births were rare.

Puritans also placed great importance on the ability to read, since they believed everyone should be able to read the Bible, God's word, himself. As a result, New England was ahead of the other colonies educationally and enjoyed extremely widespread literacy.

Since New England's climate and soil were unsuited to large-scale farming, the region developed a prosperous economy based on small farming, home industry, fishing, and especially trade and a large shipbuilding industry. Boston became a major international port.

Life in the Chesapeake colonies was drastically different. The typical Chesapeake colonist lived a shorter, less healthy life than his New England counterpart and was survived by fewer children. As a result the Chesapeake's population steadily declined despite a constant influx of settlers.

Nor was Chesapeake society as stable as that of New England. Most Chesapeake settlers came as indentured servants; and since planters desired primarily male servants for work in the tobacco fields, men largely outnumbered women in Virginia and Maryland. This hindered the development of family life. The short lifespans also contributed to the region's unstable family life as few children reached adulthood without experiencing the death of one or both parents. Remarriage resulted in households that contained children from several different marriages.

The system of indentured servitude was open to serious abuse, with masters sometimes treating their servants brutally or contriving through some technicality to lengthen their terms of indenture. In any case, forty percent of Chesapeake region indentured servants failed to survive long enough to gain their freedom.

The Chesapeake economy remained tied to the production of the region's staple crop, tobacco.

By the late seventeenth century life in the Chesapeake was beginning to stabilize, with death rates declining and life expectancies rising, though not to the New England standard. As society stabilized, an elite group of wealthy families such as the Byrds, Carters, Fitzhughs, Lees, and Randolphs, among others, began to dominate the social and political life of the region. Aping the lifestyle of the English country gentry, they built lavish manor houses from which to rule their vast plantations.

For every one of these, however, there were many small farmers who worked hard for a living, showed deference to the great planters, and hoped someday they, or their children, might reach that level.

On the bottom rung of Southern society were the black slaves. During the first half of the seventeenth century blacks in the Chesapeake made up only a small percentage of the population and were treated more or less as indentured servants. In the decades between 1640 and 1670 this gradually changed and blacks came to be seen and treated as life-long chattel slaves whose status would be inherited by their children. Larger numbers of them began to be imported and with this and rapid natural population growth they came by 1750 to compose 30 to 40 percent of the Chesapeake population.

While North Carolina tended to follow Virginia in its economic and social development (although with fewer great planters and more small farmers), South Carolina developed a society even more dominated by large plantations and chattel slavery. By the early decades of the eighteenth century blacks had come to outnumber whites in that colony. South Carolina's economy remained dependent on the cultivation of its two staple crops, rice and, to a lesser extent, indigo.

## 3.2 MERCANTILISM AND THE NAVIGATION ACTS

Beginning around 1650, British authorities began to take more interest in regulating American trade for the benefit of the mother country. A key idea that underlay this policy was the concept of mercantilism.

Mercantilists believed the world's wealth was sharply limited, and therefore one nation's gain was automatically another nation's loss. Each nation's goal was to export more than it imported (i.e., to have a "favorable balance of trade"). The difference would be made up in gold and silver, which, so the theory ran, would make the nation strong both economically and militarily. The latter was especially important since war was an integral part of the mercantilist system.

To achieve their goals, mercantilists believed economic activity should be regulated by the government.

Colonies could fit into England's mercantilist scheme by providing staple crops, such as rice, tobacco, sugar, and indigo, and raw materials, such as timber, that England would otherwise have been forced to import from other countries.

To make the colonies serve this purpose Parliament passed a series of Navigation Acts (1651, 1660, 1663, and 1673). These were the foundation of England's worldwide commercial system and some of the most important pieces of imperial legislation during the colonial period. They were also intended as weapons in England's on-going struggle against its chief seventeenth-century maritime rival, Holland. The system created by the Navigation Acts had three main provisions:

1) Trade with the colonies was to be carried on only in ships made in Britain or America and with at least 75 percent British or American crews.

2) When certain "enumerated" goods were shipped from an American port, they were to go only to Britain or to another American port.

3) Almost nothing could be imported to the colonies without going through Britain first.

Mercantilism's results were mixed. Though ostensibly for the benefit of all subjects of the British Empire, its provisions benefited some at the expense of others. It boosted the prosperity of New Englanders, who engaged in large-scale shipbuilding (something Britain's mercantilist policy-makers chose to encourage), while it hurt the residents of the Chesapeake by driving down the price of tobacco (an enumerated item). On the whole, the Navigation Acts, as intended, transferred wealth from America to Britain by increasing the prices Americans had to pay for British goods and lowering the prices Americans received for the goods they produced.

Mercantilism also helped bring on a series of three wars between England and Holland in the late 1600s.

## 3.3  BACON'S REBELLION

Charles II and his advisors worked to tighten up the administration of colonies, particularly the enforcement of the

Navigation Acts. In Virginia tempers grew short as tobacco prices plunged as a result.

Virginians were also angry at royal governor Sir William Berkeley, whose high-handed, high-taxing ways they despised and whom they believed was running the colony for the benefit of himself and his circle of cronies.

When in 1674, an impoverished nobleman of shady past by the name of Nathaniel Bacon came to Virginia and failed to gain admittance to Berkeley's inner circle with its financial advantages, he began to oppose Berkeley at every turn and came to head a faction of like-minded persons.

In 1676 disagreement over Indian policy brought the matter to the point of armed conflict. Bacon and his men burned Jamestown, but then the whole matter came to an anticlimatic ending when Bacon died of dysentery.

The British authorities, hearing of the matter, sent ships, troops, and an investigating commission. Berkeley, who had had twenty-three of the rebels hanged in reprisal, was removed; and thenceforth Virginia's royal governors had strict instructions to run the colony for the benefit of the mother country.

In response, Virginia's gentry, who had been divided over Bacon's Rebellion, united to face this new threat to their local autonomy. By political means they consistently obstructed the governors' efforts to increase royal control.

## 3.4   THE HALF-WAY COVENANT

By the latter half of the seventeenth century many Puritans were coming to fear that New England was drifting away from its religious purpose. The children and grandchildren of the first generation were displaying more concern for making money than creating a godly society.

To deal with this, some clergymen in 1662 proposed the "Half-Way Covenant," providing a sort of half-way church membership for the children of members, even though those children, having reached adulthood, did not profess saving grace as was normally required for Puritan church membership. Those who embraced the Half-Way Covenant felt that in an increasingly materialistic society it would at least keep church membership rolls full and might preserve some of the church's influence in society.

Some communities rejected the Half-Way Covenant as an improper compromise, but in general the shift toward secular values continued, though slowly. Many Puritan ministers strongly denounced this trend in sermons that have come to be referred to as "jeremiads."

## 3.5   KING PHILIP'S WAR

As New England's population grew, local Indian tribes felt threatened, and conflict sometimes resulted.

Puritans endeavored to convert Indians to Christianity. The Bible was translated into Algonquian; four villages were set up for converted Indians, who by 1650 numbered over a thousand. Still, most Indians remained unconverted.

In 1675 a Wampanoag chief named King Philip (Metacomet) led a war to exterminate the whites. Some 2,000 settlers lost their lives before King Philip was killed and his tribe subdued. New England continued to experience Indian troubles from time to time, though not as severe as those suffered by Virginia.

# 3.6   THE DOMINION OF NEW ENGLAND

The trend toward increasing imperial control of the colonies continued. In 1684 the Massachusetts charter was revoked in retaliation for that colony's large-scale evasion of the restrictions of the Navigation Acts.

The following year Charles II died and was succeeded by his brother, James II. James was prepared to go even farther in controlling the colonies, favoring the establishment of a unified government for all of New England, New York, and New Jersey. This was to be called the Dominion of New England, and the fact that it would abolish representative assemblies and facilitate the imposition of the Church of England on Congregationalist (Puritan) New England made it still more appealing to James.

To head the Dominion, James sent the obnoxious and dictatorial Sir Edmond Andros. Arriving in Boston in 1686, Andros quickly alienated the New Englanders. When news reached America of England's 1688 Glorious Revolution, replacing the Catholic James with his Protestant daughter Mary and her husband William of Orange, New Englanders cheerfully shipped Andros back to England.

Similar uprisings occurred in New York and Maryland. William and Mary's new government generally accepted these actions, though Jacob Leisler, leader of Leisler's Rebellion in New York, was executed for hesitating to turn over power to the new royal governor. This unfortunate incident poisoned the political climate of New York for many years.

The charter of Massachusetts, now including Plymouth, was restored in 1691, this time as a royal colony, though not as tightly controlled as others of that type.

## 3.7   THE SALEM WITCH TRIALS

In 1692 Massachusetts was shaken by an unusual incident in which several young girls in Salem Village (now Danvers) claimed to be tormented by the occult activities of certain of their neighbors. Before the resulting Salem witch trials could be stopped by the intervention of Puritan ministers such as Cotton Mather, some twenty persons had been executed (nineteen by hanging and one crushed under a pile of rocks).

## 3.8   PENNSYLVANIA AND DELAWARE

Pennsylvania was founded as a refuge for Quakers. One of a number of radical religious sects that had sprung up about the time of the English Civil War, the Quakers held many controversial beliefs. They believed all persons had an "inner light" which allowed them to commune directly with God. They believed human institutions were, for the most part, unnecessary and, since they believed they could receive revelation directly from God, placed little importance on the Bible. They were also pacifists and declined to show customary deference to those who were considered to be their social superiors. This and their aggressiveness in denouncing established institutions brought them trouble in both Britain and America.

William Penn, a member of a prominent British family, converted to Quakerism as a young man. Desiring to found a colony as a refuge for Quakers, in 1681 he sought and received from Charles II a grant of land in America as payment of a large debt the king had owed Penn's late father.

Penn advertised his colony widely in Europe, offered generous terms on land, and guaranteed a representative assembly and full religious freedom. He personally went to America to set up his colony, laying out the city of Philadelphia. He succeeded in maintaining peaceful relations with the Indians.

In the years that followed settlers flocked to Pennsylvania from all over Europe. The colony grew and prospered and its fertile soil made it not only attractive to settlers, but also a large exporter of grain to Europe and the West Indies.

Still, Penn's hope for an earthly Utopia was disappointed as natural dissension and wantonness asserted themselves to a certain extent even in the Quaker commonwealth.

Delaware, though at first part of Pennsylvania, was granted by Penn a separate legislature, but until the Revolution, Pennsylvania's proprietary governors also functioned as governor of Delaware.

# CHAPTER 4

# THE EIGHTEENTH CENTURY

## 4.1  ECONOMY AND POPULATION

British authorities continued to regulate the colonial economy, though usually without going so far as to provoke unrest. An exception was the Molasses Act of 1733, which would have been disastrous for New England merchants. In this case trouble was averted by the customs agents wisely declining to enforce the act stringently.

The constant drain of wealth from America to Britain, created by the mother country's mercantilistic policies, led to a corresponding drain in hard currency (gold and silver). The artificially low prices that this shortage of money created for American goods was even more advantageous to British buyers. When colonial legislatures responded by endeavoring to create paper money, British authorities blocked such moves.

Despite these hindrances, the colonial American economy remained for the most part extremely prosperous.

America's population continued to grow rapidly, both from natural increases due to prosperity and a healthy environment, and from large-scale immigration, not only of English but also of such other groups as Scots-Irish and Germans.

The Germans were prompted to migrate by wars, poverty, and religious persecution in their homeland. They found Pennsylvania especially attractive and there settled fairly close to the frontier, where land was more readily available. They eventually came to be called the "Pennsylvania Dutch."

The Scots-Irish, Scottish Presbyterians who had been living in northern Ireland for several generations, left their homes because of high rent and economic depression. In America they settled even farther west than the Germans, on or beyond the frontier in the Appalachians. They spread southward into the mountain valleys of Virginia and North Carolina.

## 4.2    THE EARLY WARS OF EMPIRE

Between 1689 and 1763 Britain and its American colonies fought a series of four wars with Spain, France, and France's Indian allies, in part to determine who would dominate North America.

Though the first war, known in America as King William's War (1689 – 1697) but in Europe as the War of the League of Augsburg, was a limited conflict involving no major battles in America, it did bring a number of bloody and terrifying border raids by Indians. It was ended by the Treaty of Ryswick, which made no major territorial changes.

The second war was known in America as Queen Anne's War (1702 – 1713), but in Europe as the War of the Spanish Succession, and brought America twelve years of sporadic

# KING GEORGE'S WAR

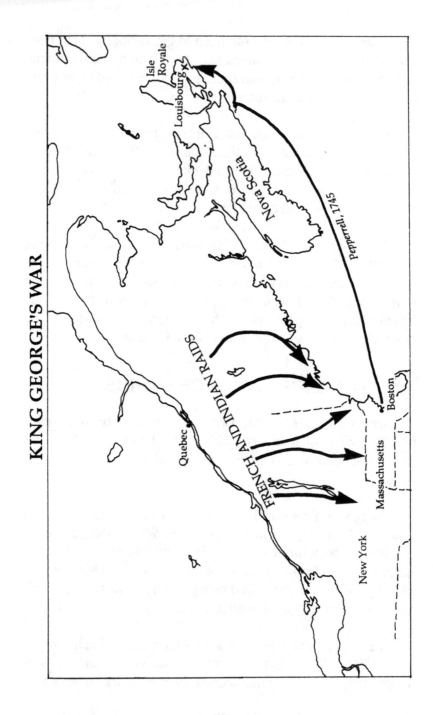

Isle Royale

Louisbourg

Nova Scotia

Pepperrell, 1745

Quebec

FRENCH AND INDIAN RAIDS

Boston

Massachusetts

New York

fighting against France and Spain. It was ended by the Treaty of Utrecht, the terms of which gave Britain major territorial gains and trade advantages.

In 1739 war once again broke out with France and Spain. Known in America as King George's war, it was called the War of Jenkin's Ear in Europe and later the War of the Austrian Succession. American troops played an active role, accompanying the British on several important expeditions and suffering thousands of casualties. In 1745 an all New England army, led by William Pepperrell, captured the powerful French fortress of Louisbourg at the mouth of the St. Lawrence River. To the Americans' disgust, the British in the 1748 Treaty of Aix-la-Chapelle gave Louisbourg back to France in exchange for lands in India.

## 4.3   GEORGIA

With this almost constant imperial warfare in mind, it was decided to found a colony as a buffer between South Carolina and Spanish-held Florida. A group of British philanthropists, led by General James Oglethorpe, in 1732 obtained a charter for such a colony, to be located between the Savannah and Altamaha Rivers and to be populated by such poor as could not manage to make a living in Great Britain.

The philanthropist trustees, who were to control the colony for twenty-one years before it reverted to royal authority, made elaborate and detailed rules to mold the new colony's society as they felt best. As a result, relatively few settlers came, and those who did complained endlessly. By 1752 Oglethorpe and his colleagues were ready to acknowledge their efforts a failure. Thereafter Georgia came to resemble South Carolina, though with more small farmers.

## 4.4 THE ENLIGHTENMENT

As the eighteenth century progressed Americans came to be more or less influenced by European ways of thought, culture, and society. Some Americans embraced the European intellectual movement known as the "Enlightenment."

The key concept of the Enlightenment was rationalism – the belief that human reason was adequate to solve all of mankind's problems and, correspondingly, much less faith was needed in the central role of God as an active force in the universe.

A major English political philosopher of the Enlightenment was John Locke. Writing partially to justify England's 1688 Glorious Revolution, he strove to find in the social and political world the sort of natural laws Isaac Newton had recently discovered in the physical realm. He held that such natural laws included the rights of life, liberty, and property; that to secure these rights people submit to governments; and that governments which abuse these rights may justly be overthrown. His writings were enormously influential in America though usually indirectly, by way of early eighteenth-century English political philosophers. Americans tended to equate Locke's law of nature with the universal law of God.

The most notable Enlightenment man in America was Benjamin Franklin. While Franklin never denied the existence of God, he focused his attention on human reason and what it could accomplish. His renown spread to Europe both for the wit and wisdom of his *Poor Richard's Almanac* and for his scientific experiments.

## 4.5   THE GREAT AWAKENING

Of much greater impact on the lives of the common people in America was the movement known as the Great Awakening. It consisted of a series of religious revivals occurring throughout the colonies from the 1720s to the 1740s. Preachers such as the Dutch Reformed Theodore Frelinghuysen, the Presbyterians William and Gilbert Tennent, and the Congregationalist Jonathan Edwards – best known for his sermon "Sinners in the Hands of an Angry God" – proclaimed a message of personal repentance and faith in Jesus Christ for salvation from an otherwise certain eternity in hell. The most dynamic preacher of the Great Awakening was the Englishman George Whitefield, who traveled through the colonies several times, speaking to crowds of up to 30,000.

The Great Awakening had several important results:

1) America's religious community came to be divided between the "Old Lights," who rejected the great Awakening, and the "New Lights," who accepted it – and sometimes suffered persecution because of their fervor.

2) A number of colleges were founded (many of them today's "Ivy League" schools), primarily for the purpose of training New-Light ministers.

3) The Great Awakening fostered a greater readiness to lay the claims of established authority – in this case religious – alongside a fixed standard – in this case the Bible – and to reject such claims it found wanting.

# 4.6  THE FRENCH AND INDIAN WAR

The Treaty of Aix-la-Chapelle (1748), ending King
George's War, provided little more than a breathing space before the next European and imperial war. England and France
continued on a collision course as France determined to take
complete control of the Ohio Valley and western Pennsylvania.

British authorities ordered colonial governors to resist this;
and Virginia's Robert Dinwiddie, already involved in specula-
tion on the Ohio Valley lands, was eager to comply. George
Washington, a young major of the Virginia militia, was sent to
western Pennsylvania to request the French to leave. When the
French declined, Washington was sent in 1754 with 200 Virginia militiamen to expel them. After success in a small skir-
mish, Washington was forced by superior numbers to fall back
on his hastily built Fort Necessity and then to surrender.

The war these operations initiated spread to Europe two
years later, where it was known as the Seven Years' War. In
America it later came to be known as the French and Indian
War.

While Washington skirmished with the French in western
Pennsylvania, delegates of seven colonies met in Albany, New
York, to discuss common plans for defense. Delegate Benjamin
Franklin proposed a plan for an intercolonial government.
While the other colonies showed no support for the idea, it was
an important precedent for the concept of uniting in the face of
a common enemy.

To deal with the French threat, the British dispatched Major
General Edward Braddock with several regiments of British
regular troops. Braddock marched overland toward the French
outpost of Fort Duquesne, at the place where the Monongahela

# THE FRENCH AND INDIAN WAR

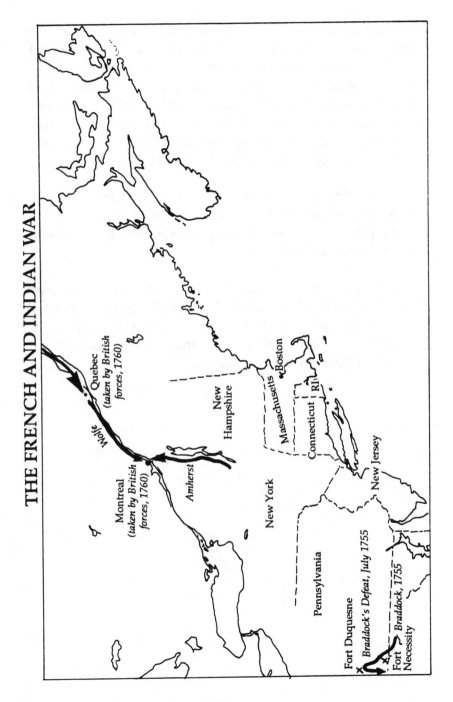

Quebec
(taken by British
forces, 1760)

Wolfe

Montreal
(taken by British
forces, 1760)

Amherst

New
Hampshire

New York

Massachusetts

Connecticut

R.I.

Boston

New Jersey

Pennsylvania

Fort Duquesne

Braddock's Defeat, July 1755

Fort
Necessity

Braddock, 1755

and Allegheny Rivers join to form the Ohio. About eight miles short of his goal he was ambushed by a small force of French and Indians. Two thirds of the British regulars, including Braddock himself, were killed. However, Britain bounced back from this humiliating defeat and several others that followed, and under the leadership of its capable and energetic prime minister, William Pitt, had by 1760 taken Quebec and Montreal and virtually liquidated the French empire in North America.

By the Treaty of Paris of 1763, which officially ended hostilities, Britain gained all of Canada and all of what is now the United States east of the Mississippi River. France lost all of its North American holdings.

Americans at the end of the French and Indian War were proud to be part of the victorious British Empire and proud of the important role they had played in making it so. They felt affection for Great Britain, and thoughts of independence would not have crossed their minds.

# CHAPTER 5

# THE COMING OF THE AMERICAN REVOLUTION

## 5.1  WRITS OF ASSISTANCE

While Americans' feelings toward Great Britain were pride and affection, British officials felt contemptuous of Americans and anxious to increase imperial control over them beyond anything that had previously been attempted. This drive to gain new authority over the colonies, beginning in 1763, led directly to American independence.

Even before that time the Writs of Assistance cases had demonstrated that Americans would not accept a reduction of their freedom.

In 1761 a young Boston lawyer named James Otis argued before a Massachusetts court that Writs of Assistance (general search warrants issued to help royal officials stop evasion of Britain's mercantilist trade restrictions) were contrary to natural law. He made his point though he lost his case, and others in the colonies joined in protesting against the Writs.

## 5.2   GRENVILLE AND THE STAMP ACT

In 1763 the strongly anti-American George Grenville became prime minister and set out to solve some of the empire's more pressing problems. Chief of these was the large national debt incurred in the recent war.

Of related concern was the cost of defending the American frontier, recently the scene of a bloody Indian uprising led by an Ottowa chief named Pontiac. Goaded by French traders, Pontiac had aimed to drive the entire white population into the sea. While failing in that endeavor, he had succeeded in killing a large number of settlers along the frontier.

Grenville created a comprehensive program to deal with these problems and moved energetically to put it into effect:

1)  He sent the Royal Navy to suppress American smuggling and enforce vigorously the Navigation Acts.

2)  He issued the Proclamation of 1763, forbidding white settlement west of the crest of the Appalachians, in hopes of keeping the Indians happy and the settlers close to the coast and thus easier to control.

3)  In 1764 he pushed through Parliament the Sugar Act (also known as the Revenue Act) aimed at raising revenue by taxes on goods imported by the Americans. It lowered by one half the duties imposed by the Molasses Act but was intended to raise revenue rather than control trade. Unlike the Molasses Act, it was stringently enforced, with accused violators facing trial in admiralty courts without benefit of jury or the normal protections of due process.

4) He determined to maintain up to 10,000 British regulars in America to control both colonists and Indians and secured passage of the Quartering Act, requiring the colonies in which British troops were stationed to pay for their maintenance. Americans had never before been required to support a standing army in their midst.

5) His Currency Act of 1764 forbade once and for all any colonial attempts to issue currency not redeemable in gold or silver, making it more difficult for Americans to avoid the constant drain of money that Britain's mercantilist policies were designed to create in the colonies.

6) Most important, however, Grenville got Parliament to pass the Stamp Act (1765), imposing a direct tax on Americans for the first time.

The Stamp Act required Americans to purchase revenue stamps on everything from newspapers to legal documents and would have created an impossible drain on hard currency in the colonies. Because it overlooked the advantage already provided by Britain's mercantilist exploitation of the colonies, Grenville's policy was shortsighted and foolish; but few in Parliament were inclined to see this.

Americans reacted first with restrained and respectful petitions and pamphlets, in which they pointed out that "taxation without representation is tyranny." From there resistance progressed to stronger and stronger protests that eventually became violent and involved intimidation of those Americans who had contracted to be the agents for distributing the stamps.

Resistance was particularly intense in Massachusetts, where it was led first by James Otis and then by Samuel Adams who formed the organization known as the Sons of Liberty.

Other colonies copied Massachusetts' successful tactics while adding some of their own. In Virginia, a young Burgess named Patrick Henry introduced seven resolutions denouncing the Stamp Act. Though only the four most moderate of them were passed by the House of Burgesses, newspapers picked up all seven and circulated them widely through the colonies, giving the impression all seven had been adopted. By their denial of Parliament's authority to tax the colonies they encouraged other colonial legislatures to issue strongly worded statements.

In October, 1765, delegates from nine colonies met as the Stamp Act Congress. Called by the Massachusetts legislature at the instigation of James Otis, the Stamp Act Congress passed moderate resolutions against the act, asserting that Americans could not be taxed without their consent, given by their representatives. They pointed out that Americans were not, and because of their location could not practically be, represented in Parliament and concluded by calling for the repeal of both the Stamp and Sugar Acts. Most important, however, the Stamp Act Congress showed that representatives of the colonies could work together and gave political leaders in the various colonies a chance to become acquainted with each other.

Most effective in achieving repeal of the Stamp Act was colonial merchants' non-importation (boycott) of British goods. Begun as an agreement among New York merchants, the boycott spread throughout the colonies and had a powerful effect on British merchants and manufacturers, who began clamoring for the act's repeal.

Meanwhile, the fickle King George III had dismissed Grenville over an unrelated disagreement and replaced him with a cabinet headed by Charles Lord Rockingham. In March, 1766, under the leadership of the new ministry, Parliament repealed the Stamp Act. At the same time, however, it passed the Declaratory Act, claiming power to tax or make laws for the

Americans "in all cases whatsoever."

Though the Declaratory Act denied exactly the principle Americans had just been at such pains to assert – that of no taxation without representation – the Americans generally ignored it in their exuberant celebration of the repeal of the Stamp Act. Americans eagerly proclaimed their loyalty to Great Britain.

## 5.3   THE TOWNSHEND ACTS

The Rockingham ministry proved to be even shorter lived than that of Grenville. It was replaced with a cabinet dominated by Chancellor of the Exchequer Charles Townshend. Townshend had boasted that he could successfully tax the colonies, and in 1766 Parliament gave him his chance by passing his program of taxes on items imported into the colonies. These taxes came to be known as the Townshend Duties. Townshend mistakenly believed the Americans would accept this method while rejecting the use of direct internal taxes.

The Townshend Acts also included the use of admiralty courts to try those accused of violations, the use of writs of assistance, and the paying of customs officials out of the fines they levied. Townshend also had the New York legislature suspended for non-compliance with the Quartering Act.

American reaction was at first slow. Philadelphia lawyer John Dickinson wrote an anonymous pamphlet entitled "Letters from a Farmer in Pennsylvania," in which he pointed out in moderate terms that the Townshend Acts violated the principle of no taxation without representation and that if Parliament could suspend the New York legislature it could do the same to others. At the same time he urged a restrained response on the part of his fellow Americans.

In February 1768 the Massachusetts legislature, at the urging of Samuel Adams, passed the Massachusetts Circular Letter, reiterating Dickinson's mild arguments and urging other colonial legislatures to pass petitions calling on Parliament to repeal the acts. Had the British government done nothing the matter might have passed quietly. Instead, British authorities acted:

1) They ordered that if the letter was not withdrawn, the Massachusetts legislature should be dissolved and new elections held,

2) They forbade the other colonial legislatures to take up the matter, and

3) They also sent four regiments of troops to Boston to prevent intimidation of royal officials and intimidate the populace instead.

The last of these actions was in response to the repeated pleas of the Boston customs agents. Corrupt agents had used technicalities of the confusing and poorly written Sugar and Townshend Acts to entrap innocent merchants and line their own pockets. Mob violence had threatened when agents had seized the ship *Liberty*, belonging to Boston merchant John Hancock. Such incidents prompted the call for troops.

The sending of troops, along with the British authority's repressive response to the Massachusetts Circular Letter aroused the Americans to resistance. Non-importation was again instituted, and soon British merchants were calling on Parliament to repeal the acts. In March 1770, Parliament, under the new prime minister, Frederick Lord North, repealed all of the taxes except that on tea, which was retained to prove Parliament had the right to tax the colonies if it so desired.

By the time of the repeal, however, friction between British soldiers and Boston citizens had led to an incident in which five Bostonians were killed. Although the British soldiers had acted more or less in self-defense, Samuel Adams labeled the incident the "Boston Massacre" and publicized it widely. At their trial the British soldiers were defended by prominent Massachusetts lawyer John Adams and were acquitted on the charge of murder.

In the years that followed, American orators desiring to stir up anti-British feeling often alluded to the Boston Massacre.

## 5.4   THE RETURN OF RELATIVE PEACE

Following the repeal of the Townshend duties a period of relative peace set in. The tax on tea remained as a reminder of Parliament's claims, but it could be easily avoided by smuggling.

Much good will had been lost and colonists remained suspicious of the British government. Many Americans believed the events of the past decade to have been the work of a deliberate conspiracy to take their liberty.

Occasional incidents marred the relative peace. One such was the burning, by a sea-going mob of Rhode Islanders disguised as Indians, of the *Gaspee*, a British customs schooner that had run aground off shore. The *Gaspee*'s captain and crew had alienated Rhode Islanders by their extreme zeal for catching smugglers as well as by their theft and vandalism when ashore.

In response to this incident British authorities appointed a commission to find the guilty parties and bring them to England for trial. Though those responsible for the burning of the

*Gaspee* were never found, this action on the part of the British prompted the colonial legislatures to form committees of correspondence to communicate with each other regarding possible threats from the British government.

## 5.5 THE TEA ACT

The relative peace was brought to an end by the Tea Act of 1773.

In desperate financial condition – partially because the Americans were buying smuggled Dutch tea rather than the taxed British product – the British East India Company sought and obtained from Parliament concessions allowing it to ship tea directly to the colonies rather than only by way of Britain. The result would be that East India Company tea, even with the tax, would be cheaper than smuggled Dutch tea. The colonists would thus, it was hoped, buy the tea, tax and all. The East India Company would be saved and the Americans would be tacitly accepting Parliament's right to tax them.

The Americans, however, proved resistant to this approach; and rather than seem to admit Parliament's right to tax, they vigorously resisted the cheaper tea. Various methods, including tar and feathers, were used to prevent the collection of the tax on tea. In most ports Americans did not allow the tea to be landed.

In Boston, however, pro-British Governor Thomas Hutchinson forced a confrontation by ordering Royal Navy vessels to prevent the tea ships from leaving the harbor. After twenty days this would, by law, result in the cargoes being sold at auction and the tax paid. The night before the time was to expire, December 16, 1773, Bostonians thinly disguised as Indians boarded the ships and threw the tea into the harbor.

Many Americans felt this – the destruction of private property – was going too far, but the reaction of Lord North and Parliament quickly united Americans in support of Boston and opposition to Britain.

## 5.6    THE INTOLERABLE ACTS

The British responded with four acts collectively titled the Coercive Acts:

1) The Boston Port Act closed the port of Boston to all trade until local citizens would agree to pay for the lost tea (they would not).

2) The Massachusetts Government Act greatly increased the power of Massachusetts' royal governor at the expense of the legislature.

3) The Administration of Justice Act provided that royal officials accused of crimes in Massachusetts could be tried elsewhere, where chances of acquittal might be greater.

4) A strengthened Quartering Act allowed the new governor, General Thomas Gage, to quarter his troops anywhere, including unoccupied private homes.

A further act of Parliament also angered and alarmed Americans. This was the Quebec Act, which extended the province of Quebec to the Ohio River, established Roman Catholicism as Quebec's official religion, and set up for Quebec a government without a representative assembly.

For Americans this was a denial of the hopes and expectations of westward expansion for which they had fought the French and Indian War. Also, New Englanders especially saw it as a threat that in their colonies too, Parliament could establish autocratic government and the hated Church of England.

Americans lumped the Quebec Act together with the Coercive Acts and referred to them all as the Intolerable Acts.

In response to the Coercive Acts, the First Continental Congress was called and met in Philadelphia in September, 1774. It once again petitioned Parliament for relief but also passed the Suffolk Resolves (so called because they were first passed in Suffolk County, Massachusetts), denouncing the Intolerable Acts and calling for strict non-importation and rigorous preparation of local militia companies in case the British should resort to military force.

The Congress then narrowly rejected a plan, submitted by Joseph Galloway of Pennsylvania, calling for a union of the colonies within the empire and a rearrangement of relations with Parliament. Most of the delegates felt matters had already gone too far for such a mild measure. Finally, before adjournment, it was agreed that there should be a Second Continental Congress to meet in May of the following year if the colonies' grievances had not been righted by then.

# CHAPTER 6

# THE WAR FOR INDEPENDENCE

## 6.1   LEXINGTON AND CONCORD

The British government paid little attention to the First Continental Congress, having decided to teach the Americans a military lesson. More troops were sent to Massachusetts, which was officially declared to be in a state of rebellion. Orders were sent to General Gage to arrest the leaders of the resistance or, failing that, to provoke any sort of confrontation that would allow him to turn British military might loose on the Americans.

Gage decided on a reconnaissance-in-force to find and destroy a reported stockpile of colonial arms and ammunition at Concord. Seven hundred British troops set out on this mission on the night of April 18, 1775. Their movement was detected by American surveillance and news was spread throughout the countryside by dispatch riders Paul Revere and William Dawes.

At the little village of Lexington, Captain John Parker and some seventy Minutemen (militiamen trained to respond at a moment's notice) awaited the British on the village green. As the British approached, a British officer shouted at the Minutemen to lay down their arms and disperse. The Minutemen did not lay down their arms but did turn to file off the green. A shot was fired, and then the British opened fire and charged. Eight Americans were killed and several others wounded, most shot in the back.

The British continued to Concord only to find that nearly all of the military supplies they had expected to find had already been moved. Attacked by growing numbers of Minutemen, they began to retreat toward Boston. As the British retreated, Minutemen, swarming from every village for miles around, fired on the column from behind rocks, trees, and stone fences. Only a relief force of additional British troops saved the first column from destruction.

Open warfare had begun, and the myth of British invincibility was destroyed. Militia came in large numbers from all the New England colonies to join the force besieging Gage and his army in Boston.

## 6.2 BUNKER HILL

In May, 1775, three more British generals, William Howe, Henry Clinton, and John Burgoyne, arrived in Boston urging Gage to further aggressive action. The following month the Americans tightened the noose around Boston by fortifying Breed's Hill (a spur of Bunker Hill), from which they could, if necessary, bombard Boston.

The British determined to remove them by a frontal attack that would demonstrate the awesome power of British arms.

Twice the British were thrown back and finally succeeded as the Americans ran out of ammunition. Over a thousand British soldiers were killed or wounded in what turned out to be the bloodiest battle of the war (June 17, 1775). Yet the British had gained very little and remained bottled up in Boston.

Meanwhile in May, 1775, American forces under Ethan Allen and Benedict Arnold took Fort Ticonderoga on Lake Champlain.

Congress, hoping Canada would join in resistance against Britain, authorized two expeditions into Quebec. One, under General Richard Montgomery took Montreal and then turned toward the city of Quebec. It was met there by the second expedition under Benedict Arnold. The attack on Quebec (December 31, 1775) failed, Montgomery was killed, Arnold wounded, and American hopes for Canada ended.

## 6.3 THE SECOND CONTINENTAL CONGRESS

While these events were taking place in New England and Canada, the Second Continental Congress met in Philadelphia in May, 1775. Congress was divided into two main factions:

1) One was composed mostly of New Englanders and leaned toward declaring independence from Britain.

2) The other drew its strength primarily from the Middle Colonies and was not yet ready to go that far. It was led by John Dickinson of Pennsylvania.

Congress took action to deal with the difficult situation facing the colonies. It:

1) adopted the New England army around Boston, calling on the other colonies to send troops and sending George Washington to command it,

2) adopted a "Declaration of the Causes and Necessity for Taking up Arms" and

3) adopted the "Olive Branch Petition" pleading with King George III to intercede with Parliament to restore peace.

This last overture was ignored in Britain, where the king gave his approval to the Prohibitory Act, declaring the colonies in rebellion and no longer under his protection. Preparations were made for full-scale war against America.

Throughout 1775, Americans remained deeply loyal to Britain and King George III despite the king's proclamations declaring them to be in revolt. In Congress moderates still resisted independence.

In January, 1776, Thomas Paine published a pamphlet entitled *Common Sense*, calling for immediate independence. Its arguments were extreme and sometimes illogical and its language intemperate, but it sold largely and may have had much influence in favor of independence. Continued evidence of Britain's intention to carry on the war throughout the colonies also weakened the moderates' resistance to independence. The Prohibitory Act, with its virtual declaration of war against America, convinced many that no further moral scruples need stand in the way of such a step.

On June 7, 1776, Richard Henry Lee of Virginia introduced a series of formal resolutions in Congress calling for independence and a national government. Accepting these ideas, Congress named two committees. One, headed by John Dickinson, was to work out a framework for a national government. The other was to draft a statement of the reasons for declaring independence. This statement, the Declaration of Independence, was primarily the work of Thomas Jefferson of Virginia. It was a restatement of political ideas by then commonplace in America, showing why the former colonists felt justified in separating from Great Britain. It was formally adopted by Congress on July 4, 1776.

## 6.4   WASHINGTON TAKES COMMAND

Britain meanwhile was preparing a massive effort to conquer the United States. Gage was removed as being too timid, and top command went to Howe. To supplement the British army, large numbers of troops were hired from various German principalities. Since many of these Germans came from the state of Hesse-Kassel, Americans referred to all such troops as Hessians.

Although the London authorities desired a quick and smashing campaign, General Howe and his brother, British naval commander Richard, Admiral Lord Howe, intended to move slowly, using their powerful force to cow the Americans into signing loyalty oaths.

In March, 1776, Washington placed on Dorchester Heights, overlooking Boston, some of the large cannon that had been captured at Ticonderoga, forcing the British to evacuate the city.

The British shipped their troops to Nova Scotia and then, together with large reinforcements from Britain, landed that summer at New York City. They hoped to find many loyalists there and make that city the key to their campaign to subdue America.

Washington anticipated the move and was waiting at New York, which Congress had ordered should be defended. However, the under-trained, under-equipped, and badly outnumbered American army was no match for the powerful forces under the Howes. Defeated at the Battle of Long Island (August 27, 1776), Washington narrowly avoided being trapped there (an escape partially due to the Howes' slowness). Defeated again at the Battle of Washington Heights (August 29 – 30, 1776) on Manhattan, Washington was forced to retreat across New Jersey with the aggressive British General Lord Cornwallis, a subordinate of Howe, in pursuit. By December what was left of Washington's army had made it into Pennsylvania.

With his victory almost complete, Howe decided to wait till spring to finish annihilating Washington's army. Scattering his troops in small detachments so as to hold all of New Jersey, he went into winter quarters.

Washington, with his small army melting away as demoralized soldiers deserted, decided on a bold stroke. On Christmas night 1776, his army crossed the Delaware River and struck the Hessians at Trenton. The Hessians, still groggy from their hard-drinking Christmas party, were easily defeated. A few days later Washington defeated a British force at Princeton (January 3, 1777).

Howe was so shocked by these two unexpected defeats that he pulled his outposts back close to New York. Much of New Jersey was regained. Those who had signed British loyalty oaths in the presence of Howe's army were now at the mercy of their patriot neighbors. And Washington's army was saved from disintegration.

Early in the war France began making covert shipments of

arms to the Americans. This it did, not because the French government loved freedom (it did not), but because it hated Britain and saw the war as a way to weaken Britain by depriving it of its colonies. Arms shipments from France were vital for the Americans.

## 6.5   SARATOGA AND VALLEY FORGE

For the summer of 1777 the British home authorities adopted an elaborate plan of campaign urged on them by General Burgoyne. According to the plan Burgoyne himself would lead an army southward from Canada along the Lake Champlain corridor while another army under Howe moved up the Hudson River to join hands with Burgoyne at Albany. This, it was hoped, would cut off New England and allow the British to subdue that region, which they considered the hotbed of the "rebellion."

Howe had other ideas and shipped his army by sea to Chesapeake Bay, hoping to capture the American capital, Philadelphia, and destroy Washington's army at the same time. At Brandywine Creek (September 1, 1777) Washington tried but failed to stop Howe's advance. Yet the American army, though badly beaten, remained intact. Howe occupied Philadelphia as the Congress fled westward to York, Pennsylvania.

In early October, Washington attempted to drive Howe out of Philadelphia; but his attack at Germantown, though at first successful, failed at least partially due to thick fog and the still imperfect level of training in the American army, both of which contributed to confusion among the troops. Thereafter Howe settled down to comfortable winter quarters in Philadelphia, and Washington and his army to very uncomfortable ones at nearby Valley Forge, while far to the north, the British strategy that Howe had ignored was going badly awry.

# THE AMERICAN REVOLUTION

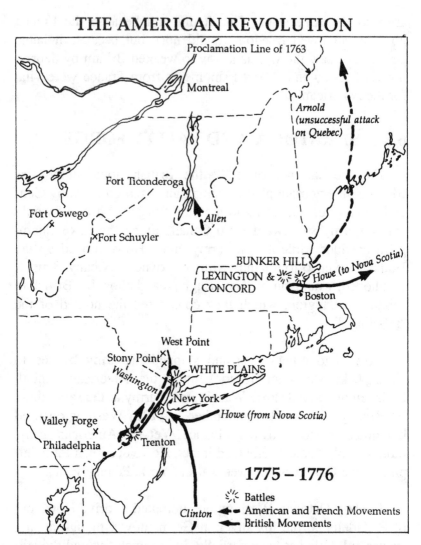

Proclamation Line of 1763

Montreal

Arnold
(unsuccessful attack
on Quebec)

Fort Ticonderoga

Fort Oswego

Fort Schuyler

Allen

BUNKER HILL
LEXINGTON &
CONCORD

Howe (to Nova Scotia)

Boston

West Point

Stony Point

Washington

WHITE PLAINS

New York

Howe (from Nova Scotia)

Valley Forge

Philadelphia

Trenton

**1775 – 1776**

Battles
American and French Movements
British Movements

Clinton

Burgoyne's advance began well but slowed as the Americans placed obstructions on the rough wilderness trails by which his army, including numerous cannon and much bulky baggage, had to advance. A diversionary force of British troops and Iroquois Indians under the command of Colonel Barry St. Leger swung east of Burgoyne's column, but although it defeated and killed American General Nicholas Herkimer at the

Battle of Oriskany (August 6, 1777), it was finally forced to withdraw to Canada.

In mid-August, a detachment of Burgoyne's force was defeated by New England militia under General John Stark near Bennington in what is now Vermont. By autumn Burgoyne found his way blocked by an American army: continentals (American regular troops such as those that made up most of Washington's army, paid, in theory at least, by Congress); and New England militia, under General Horatio Gates, at Saratoga, about thirty miles north of Albany. Burgoyne's two attempts to break through (September 19 and October 7, 1777) were turned back by the Americans under the brilliant battlefield leadership of Benedict Arnold. On October 17, 1777, Burgoyne surrendered to Gates.

The American victory at Saratoga convinced the French to join openly in the war against England. Eventually the Spanish (1779) and the Dutch (1780) joined as well, and England was faced with a world war.

## 6.6   THE BRITISH MOVE SOUTH

The new circumstances brought a change in British strategy. With fewer troops available for service in America, the British would have to depend more on loyalists, and since they imagined that larger numbers of these existed in the South than elsewhere, it was there they turned their attention.

Howe was relieved and replaced by General Henry Clinton, who was ordered to abandon Philadelphia and march to New York. In doing so, he narrowly avoided defeat at the hands of Washington's army – much improved after a winter's drilling at Valley Forge under the direction of Prussian nobleman

# THE AMERICAN REVOLUTION

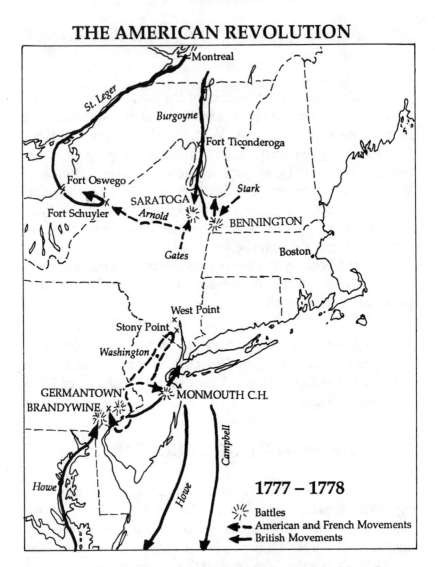

Baron von Stuben – at the Battle of Monmouth, New Jersey (June 28, 1778).

Clinton was thenceforth to maintain New York as Britain's main base in America while detaching troops to carry out the new Southern strategy. In November 1778 the British easily conquered Georgia. Late the following year Clinton moved on South Carolina with a land and naval force, and in May 1780, U.S. General Benjamin Lincoln surrendered Charleston. Clinton then returned to New York, leaving Cornwallis to continue the Southern campaign.

Congress, alarmed at the British successes, sent General Horatio Gates to lead the forces opposing Cornwallis. Gates blundered to a resounding defeat at the Battle of Camden, in South Carolina (August 16, 1780).

The general outlook seemed bad for America at that point in the war. Washington's officers grumbled about their pay in arrears. The army was understrength and then suffered successive mutinies among the Pennsylvania and New Jersey troops. Benedict Arnold went over to the British. In short, the British seemed to be winning the contest of endurance. This outlook was soon to change.

In the West, George Rogers Clark, acting under the auspices of the state of Virginia, led an expedition down the Ohio River and into the area of present-day Illinois and Indiana, defeating a British force at Vincennes, Indiana, and securing the area north of the Ohio River for the United States.

In the South, Cornwallis began to move northward toward North Carolina, but on October 7, 1780 a detachment of his force under Major Patrick Ferguson was defeated by American frontiersman at the Battle of Kings Mountain in northern South Carolina. To further increase the problems facing the British, Cornwallis had unwisely moved north without bothering to secure South Carolina first. The result was that the British would no sooner leave an area than American militia or guerilla bands, such as that under Francis Marion ("the Swamp Fox"), were once again in control and able to deal with those who had expressed loyalty to Britain in the presence of Cornwallis's army.

To command the continental forces in the South, Washington sent his most able subordinate, military genius Nathaniel Greene. Greene's brilliant strategy led to a crushing victory at Cowpens, South Carolina (January 17, 1781) by troops under Greene's subordinate, General Daniel Morgan of Virginia. It also led to a near victory by Greene's own force at Guilford Court House, North Carolina, (March 15, 1781).

## 6.7   YORKTOWN

The frustrated and impetuous Cornwallis now abandoned the Southern strategy and moved north into Virginia. Clinton, disgusted at this departure from plan, sent instructions for Cornwallis to take up a defensive position and await further orders. Against his better judgment Cornwallis did so, selecting Yorktown, Virginia, on a peninsula that reaches into Chesapeake Bay between the York and James Rivers.

Washington now saw and seized the opportunity this presented. With the aid of a French fleet which took control of Chesapeake Bay and a French army that joined him in sealing off the land approaches to Yorktown, Washington succeeded in trapping Cornwallis. After three weeks of siege, Cornwallis surrendered, October 17, 1781.

## 6.8   THE WAR AT SEA

Britain had other problems as well. Ships of the small but daring U.S. Navy as well as privateers (privately owned vessels outfitted with guns and authorized by a warring government to capture enemy merchant ships for profit) preyed on the British

# THE AMERICAN REVOLUTION

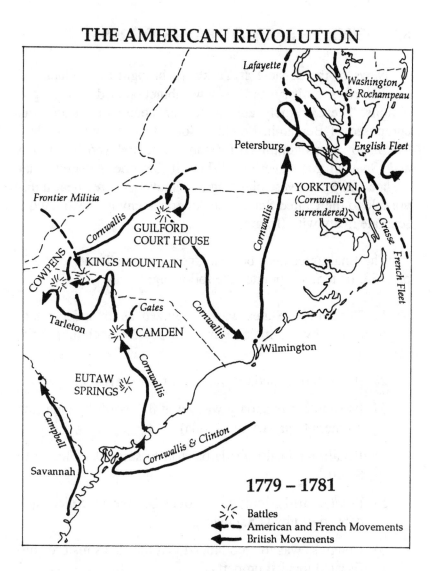

Lafayette

Washington & Rochampeau

Petersburg

English Fleet

YORKTOWN
(Cornwallis surrendered)

Frontier Militia

Cornwallis

Cornwallis

De Grasse

French Fleet

GUILFORD
COURT HOUSE

COWPENS

KINGS MOUNTAIN

Tarleton

Gates

Cornwallis

CAMDEN

Wilmington

Campbell

EUTAW
SPRINGS

Cornwallis

Savannah

Cornwallis & Clinton

**1779 – 1781**

Battles
American and French Movements
British Movements

merchant marine. John Paul Jones, the most famous of American naval leaders, captured ships and carried out audacious raids along the coast of Britain itself.

French and Spanish naval forces also struck against various outposts of the British Empire.

# 6.9  THE TREATY OF PARIS OF 1783

News of the debacle at Yorktown brought the collapse of Lord North's ministry, and the new cabinet opened peace negotiations. The extremely able American negotiating team was composed of Benjamin Franklin, John Adams, and John Jay. The negotiations continued for some time, delayed by French and Spanish maneuvering. When it became apparent that France and Spain were planning to achieve an agreement unfavorable to the United States, the American envoys negotiated a separate treaty with Britain.

The final agreement became known as the Treaty of Paris of 1783. Its terms stipulated the following:

1) The United States was recognized as an independent nation by the major European powers, including Britain.

2) Its western boundary was set at the Mississippi River.

3) Its southern boundary was set at 31° north latitude (the northern boundary of Florida).

4) Britain retained Canada but had to surrender Florida to Spain.

5) Private British creditors would be free to collect any debts owed by U.S. citizens.

6) Congress was to recommend that the states restore confiscated loyalist property.

# CHAPTER 7

# THE CREATION OF NEW GOVERNMENTS

## 7.1   THE STATE CONSTITUTIONS

After the collapse of British authority in 1775, it became necessary to form new state governments. By the end of 1777 ten new state constitutions had been formed.

Connecticut and Rhode Island kept their colonial charters, which were republican in nature, simply deleting references to British sovereignty. Massachusetts waited until 1780 to complete the adoption of its new constitution. The constitutions ranged from such extremely democratic models as the virtually unworkable Pennsylvania constitution (soon abandoned), in which a unicameral legislature ruled with little check or balance, to more reasonable frameworks such as those of Maryland and Virginia, which included more safeguards against popular excesses.

Massachusetts voters set an important example by insisting that a constitution should be made by a special convention rather than the legislature. This would make the constitution superior to the legislature and, hopefully, assure that the legislature would be subject to the constitution.

Most state constitutions included bills of rights – lists of things the government was not supposed to do to the people.

## 7.2   THE ARTICLES OF CONFEDERATION

In the summer of 1776, Congress appointed a committee to begin devising a framework for national government. When completed, this document was known as the Articles of Confederation. John Dickinson, who had played a leading role in writing the Articles, felt a strong national government was needed; but by the time Congress finished revising them, the Articles went to the opposite extreme of preserving the sovereignty of the states and creating a very weak national government.

The Articles of Confederation provided for a unicameral Congress in which each state would have one vote, as had been the case in the Continental Congress. Executive authority under the Articles would be vested in a committee of thirteen, one member from each state. In order to amend the Articles, the unanimous consent of all the states was required. The Articles of Confederation government was empowered to do the following:

1)   make war,

2)   make treaties,

3)   determine the amount of troops and money each state should contribute to the war effort,

4)   settle disputes between states,

5)  admit new states to the Union, and

6)  borrow money.

More importantly, however, was that it was not empowered to do the following:

1)  levy taxes,

2)  raise troops, or

3)  regulate commerce.

Ratification of the Articles of Confederation was delayed by a disagreement over the future status of the lands that lay to the west of the original thirteen states. Some states, notably Virginia, held extensive claims to these lands based on their original colonial charters. Maryland, which had no such claim, withheld ratification until in 1781 Virginia agreed to surrender its western claims to the new national government.

Meanwhile, the country was on its way to deep financial trouble. Unable to tax, Congress resorted to printing large amounts of paper money to finance the war; but these inflated "Continentals" were soon worthless. Other financial schemes fell through, and only grants and loans from France and the Netherlands staved off complete financial collapse. A plan to amend the Articles to give Congress power to tax was stopped by the lone opposition of Rhode Island. The army, whose pay was far in arrears, threatened mutiny. Some of those who favored a stronger national government welcomed this development and in what became known as the Newburgh Conspiracy (1783) consulted with army second-in-command Horatio Gates as to the possibility of using the army to force the states to surrender more power to the national government. This movement was stopped by a moving appeal to the officers by Washington himself.

## 7.3 THE TRANS-APPALACHIAN WEST AND THE NORTHWEST ORDINANCE

For many Americans the enormous trans-Appalachian frontier represented an opportunity to escape the economic hard times that followed the end of the war.

In 1775, Daniel Boone opened the "Wilderness Road" through the Cumberland Gap and on to the "Bluegrass" region of Kentucky. Others scouted down the Ohio River from Pittsburgh. By 1790, over 100,000 had settled in Kentucky and Tennessee, despite the risk of violent death at the hands of Indians. This risk was made worse by the presence of the British in northwestern military posts that should have been evacuated at the end of the war. From these posts they supplied the Indians with guns and encouraged them to use them on Americans. The Spaniards on the Florida frontier behaved in much the same way.

The settlement of Kentucky and Tennessee increased the pressure for the opening of the lands north of the Ohio River. To facilitate this Congress passed three land ordinances in the years from 1784 to 1787.

1) The Land Ordinance of 1784 provided for territorial government and an orderly system by which each territory could progress to full statehood (this ordinance is sometimes considered part of the Land Ordinance of 1785).

2) The Land Ordinance of 1785 provided for the orderly surveying and distribution of land in townships six miles square, each composed of thirty-six one-square-mile (640 acre) sections, of which one should be set aside for the support of education. (This ordinance is

sometimes referred to as the "Northwest Ordinance of 1785").

3) The Northwest Ordinance of 1787 provided a bill of rights for settlers and forbade slavery north of the Ohio River.

These ordinances were probably the most important legislation of the Articles of Confederation government.

## 7.4    THE JAY-GARDOQUI NEGOTIATIONS

Economic depression followed the end of the war as the United States remained locked into the disadvantageous commercial system of the British Empire but without the trade advantages that system had provided.

One man who thought he saw a way out of the economic quagmire was Congress's secretary of foreign affairs, John Jay. In 1784, Jay began negotiating with Spanish minister Gardoqui a treaty that would have granted lucrative commercial privileges – benefiting large east-coast merchants such as Jay – in exchange for U.S. acceptance of Spain's closure of the Mississippi River as an outlet for the agricultural goods of the rapidly growing settlements in Kentucky and Tennessee. This the Spanish desired because they feared that extensive settlement in what was then the western part of the United States might lead to American hunger for Spanish-held lands.

When Jay reported this to Congress in the summer of 1786, the West and South were outraged. Negotiations were broken off. Some, angered that Jay could show so little concern for the other sections of the country, talked of dissolving the Union; and this helped spur to action those who desired not the dissolution but the strengthening of the Union.

## 7.5   SHAYS' REBELLION

Nationalists were further stimulated to action by Shays' Rebellion (1786). Economic hard times coupled with high taxes intended to pay off the state's war debt drove western Massachusetts farmers to desperation. Led by war veteran Daniel Shays, they shut down courts to prevent judges from seizing property or condemning people to debtors' prison for failing to pay their taxes.

The unrest created a disproportionate amount of panic in the rest of the state and the nation. The citizens of Boston subscribed money to raise an army to suppress the rebels. The success of this army together with timely tax relief caused the "rebellion" to fizzle out fairly quickly.

Amid the panic caused by the news of the uprising, many came to feel that a stronger government was needed to control such violent public outbursts as those of the western Massachusetts farmers.

## 7.6   TOWARD A NEW CONSTITUTION

As time went on the inadequacy of the Articles of Confederation became increasingly apparent. Congress could not compel the states to comply with the terms of the Treaty of Paris of 1783 regarding debts and loyalists' property. The British used this as an excuse for not evacuating their Northwestern posts, hoping to be on hand to make the most of the situation when, as they not unreasonably expected, the new government fell to pieces. In any case, Congress could do nothing to force them out of the posts, nor to solve any of the nation's other increasingly pressing problems.

In these dismal straits, some called for disunion, others for monarchy. Still others felt that republican government could still work if given a better constitution, and they made it their goal to achieve this.

In 1785 a meeting of representatives of Virginia, Maryland, Pennsylvania, and Delaware was held at George Washington's residence, Mt. Vernon, for the purpose of discussing current problems of interstate commerce. At their suggestion the Virginia legislature issued a call for a convention of all the states on the same subject, to meet the following summer in Annapolis, Maryland.

The Annapolis Convention met in September of 1786, but only five states were represented. Among those present, however, were such nationalists as Alexander Hamilton, John Dickinson, and James Madison. With so few states represented it was decided instead to call for a convention of all the states to meet the following summer in Philadelphia for the purpose of revising the Articles of Confederation.

# 7.7   THE CONSTITUTIONAL CONVENTION

The men who met in Philadelphia in 1787 were remarkably able, highly educated, and exceptionally accomplished. For the most part they were lawyers, merchants and planters. Though representing individual states, most thought in national terms. Prominent among them were James Madison, Alexander Hamilton, Gouvernor Morris, Robert Morris, John Dickinson, and Benjamin Franklin.

George Washington was unanimously elected to preside, and the enormous respect that he commanded helped hold the convention together through difficult times (as it had the Continental Army) and make the product of the convention's work more attractive to the rest of the nation. The delegates then voted that the convention's discussions should be secret, to avoid the distorting and confusing influence of the press and publicity.

The delegates shared a basic belief in the innate selfishness of man, which must somehow be kept from abusing the power of government. For this purpose the document that they finally produced contained many checks and balances, designed to prevent the government, or any one branch of the government, from gaining too much power.

Madison, who has been called the "father of the Constitution," devised a plan of national government and persuaded fellow Virginian Edmund Randolph, who was more skilled at public speaking, to introduce it. Known as the "Virginia Plan," it called for an executive branch and two houses of Congress, each based on population.

Smaller states, who would thus have seen their influence decreased, objected and countered with William Patterson's "New Jersey Plan," calling for the continuation of a unicameral legislature with equal representation for the states as well as sharply increased powers for the national government.

A temporary impasse developed that threatened to break up the convention. At this point Benjamin Franklin played an important role in reconciling the often heated delegates, suggesting that the sessions of the convention henceforth begin with prayer (they did) and making various other suggestions that eventually helped the convention arrive at the "Great Compromise." The Great Compromise provided for a Presidency, a Senate with all states represented equally (by two Senators each), and a House of Representatives with representation according to population.

Another crisis involved North-South disagreement over the issue of slavery. Here also a compromise was reached. Slavery was neither endorsed nor condemned by the Constitution. Each slave was to count as three fifths of a person for purposes of apportioning representation and direct taxation on the states (the Three-Fifths Compromise). The federal government was prohibited from stopping the importation of slaves prior to 1808.

The third major area of compromise was the nature of the Presidency. This was made easier by the virtual certainty that George Washington would be the first president and the universal trust that he would not abuse the powers of the office or set a bad example for his successors. The result was a strong Presidency with control of foreign policy and the power to veto Congress's legislation. Should the president commit an actual crime, Congress would have the power to impeach him. Otherwise the president would serve for a term of four years and be re-electable without limit. As a check to the possible excesses of democracy, the president was to be elected by an Electoral College, in which each state would have the same number of electors as it did Senators and Representatives combined. The person with the second highest total in the Electoral College would be Vice-President. If no one gained a majority in the Electoral College, the President would be chosen by the House of Representatives.

The new Constitution was to take effect when nine states, through special state conventions, had ratified it.

## 7.8    THE STRUGGLE FOR RATIFICATION

As the struggle over ratification got under way, those favoring the Constitution astutely took for themselves the name Federalists (i.e., advocates of centralized power) and labeled their opponents Anti-Federalists. The Federalists were effective in explaining the convention and the document it had produced. *The Federalist Papers*, written as a series of eighty-five newspaper articles by Alexander Hamilton, James Madison, and John Jay, brilliantly expounded the Constitution and demonstrated how it was designed to prevent the abuse of power from any direction. These essays are considered to be the best commentary on the Constitution by those who helped write it.

At first, ratification progressed smoothly, with five states approving in quick succession. In Massachusetts, however, a tough fight developed. By skillful maneuvering, Federalists were able to win over to their side such popular opponents of the Constitution as Samuel Adams and John Hancock. Others were won over by the promise that a bill of rights would be added to the Constitution, limiting the federal government just as the state governments were limited by their bills of rights. With such promises, Massachusetts ratified by a narrow margin.

By June 21, 1788, the required nine states had ratified, but the crucial states of New York and Virginia still held out. In Virginia, where George Mason and Patrick Henry opposed the Constitution, the influence of George Washington and the promise of a bill of rights finally prevailed and ratification was achieved there as well. In New York, where Alexander Hamilton led the fight for ratification, *The Federalist Papers*, the promise of a bill of rights, and the news of Virginia's ratification were enough to carry the day.

Only North Carolina and Rhode Island still held out, but they both ratified within the next fifteen months.

In March, 1789, George Washington was inaugurated as the nation's first president.

# THE BEST TEST PREPARATION FOR THE

# GRE

**GRADUATE**
**RECORD**
**EXAMINATION**

# HISTORY

by Niles R. Holt, Ph.D. • Gary Pagram, Ph.D. •
William T. Walker, Ph.D. • Steven Wordsworth, Ph.D.

## 3 Full-Length Exams

**Completely Up-to-Date** based on the current format of the GRE History Test

➤ The ONLY test preparation book with detailed explanations to every exam question

➤ Far more comprehensive than any other test preparation book

**Includes a COMPREHENSIVE HISTORY REVIEW, emphasizing all major topics found on the exam**

*Research & Education Association*

*Available at your local bookstore or order directly from us by sending in coupon below.*

---

**RESEARCH & EDUCATION ASSOCIATION**
61 Ethel Road W. • Piscataway, New Jersey 08854
Phone: (732) 819-8880

**VISA** | **MasterCard**

☐ Payment enclosed
☐ Visa ☐ Master Card

Charge Card Number

Expiration Date: _____ / _____
Mo          Yr

Please ship **"GRE History"** @ $26.95 plus $4.00 for shipping.

Name _____

Address _____

City _____ State _____ Zip _____

REA's
# HANDBOOK OF
# ENGLISH
## Grammar, Style, and Writing

**All the essentials that you need are contained in this simple and practical book**

*Learn quickly and easily all you need to know about*

- Rules and exceptions in grammar
- Spelling and proper punctuation
- Common errors in sentence structure
- Correct usage from 2,000 examples
- Effective writing skills

*Complete practice exercises with answers follow each chapter*

**REA** RESEARCH & EDUCATION ASSOCIATION

*Available at your local bookstore or order directly from us by sending in coupon below.*

**RESEARCH & EDUCATION ASSOCIATION**
61 Ethel Road W., Piscataway, New Jersey 08854
Phone: (732) 819-8880

□ Payment enclosed
□ Visa  □ Master Card

Charge Card Number

Expiration Date: _____ / _____
Mo        Yr

Please ship **"Handbook of English"** @ $19.95 plus $4.00 for shipping.

Name _____

Address _____

City _____ State _____ Zip _____

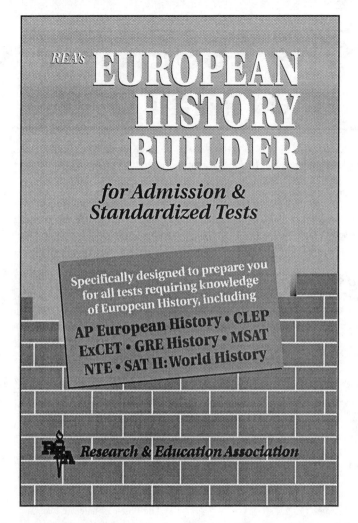

**REA's EUROPEAN HISTORY BUILDER**

**for Admission & Standardized Tests**

Specifically designed to prepare you for all tests requiring knowledge of European History, including

**AP European History • CLEP ExCET • GRE History • MSAT NTE • SAT II: World History**

**Research & Education Association**

*Available at your local bookstore or order directly from us by sending in coupon below.*

---

RESEARCH & EDUCATION ASSOCIATION
61 Ethel Road W., Piscataway, New Jersey 08854
Phone: (732) 819-8880

VISA     MasterCard

☐ Payment enclosed
☐ Visa   ☐ Master Card

Charge Card Number

Expiration Date: _____ / _____
                    Mo        Yr

Please ship **REA's EUROPEAN HISTORY BUILDER** @ $14.95 plus $4.00 for shipping.

Name _____

Address _____

City _____ State _____ Zip _____

# "The ESSENTIALS" of HISTORY

REA's **Essentials of History** series offers a new approach to the study of history that is different from what has been available previously. Compared with conventional history outlines, the **Essentials of History** offer far more detail, with fuller explanations and interpretations of historical events and developments. Compared with voluminous historical tomes and textbooks, the **Essentials of History** offer a far more concise, less ponderous overview of each of the periods they cover.

The **Essentials of History** provide quick access to needed information, and will serve as a handy reference source at all times. The **Essentials of History** are prepared with REA's customary concern for high professional quality and student needs.

## UNITED STATES HISTORY

**1500 to 1789** From Colony to Republic
**1789 to 1841** The Developing Nation
**1841 to 1877** Westward Expansion & the Civil War
**1877 to 1912** Industrialism, Foreign Expansion & the Progressive Era
**1912 to 1941** World War I, the Depression & the New Deal
**America since 1941:** Emergence as a World Power

## WORLD HISTORY

**Ancient History (4,500 BC to AD 500)**
The Emergence of Western Civilization
**Medieval History (AD 500 to 1450)**
The Middle Ages

## EUROPEAN HISTORY

**1450 to 1648** The Renaissance, Reformation & Wars of Religion
**1648 to 1789** Bourbon, Baroque & the Enlightenment
**1789 to 1848** Revolution & the New European Order
**1848 to 1914** Realism & Materialism
**1914 to 1935** World War I & Europe in Crisis
**Europe since 1935:** From World War II to the Demise of Communism

## CANADIAN HISTORY

**Pre-Colonization to 1867**
The Beginning of a Nation
**1867 to Present**
The Post-Confederate Nation

*If you would like more information about any of these books,*
*complete the coupon below and return it to us or visit your local bookstore.*

---

**RESEARCH & EDUCATION ASSOCIATION**
61 Ethel Road W. • Piscataway, New Jersey 08854
Phone: (732) 819-8880

**Please send me more information about your History Essentials books**

Name _____

Address _____

City _____ State _____ Zip _____

# REA's Test Preps
# The Best in Test Preparation

- REA "Test Preps" are **far more** comprehensive than any other test preparation series
- Each book contains up to **eight** full-length practice exams based on the most recent exams
- **Every** type of question likely to be given on the exams is included
- Answers are accompanied by **full** and **detailed** explanations

*REA has published over 60 Test Preparation volumes in several series. They include:*

**Advanced Placement Exams (APs)**
Biology
Calculus AB & Calculus BC
Chemistry
Computer Science
English Language & Composition
English Literature & Composition
European History
Government & Politics
Physics
Psychology
Statistics
Spanish Language
United States History

**College-Level Examination Program (CLEP)**
Analysis & Interpretation of Literature
College Algebra
Freshman College Composition
General Examinations
General Examinations Review
History of the United States I
Human Growth and Development
Introductory Sociology
Principles of Marketing
Spanish

**SAT II: Subject Tests**
American History
Biology
Chemistry
English Language Proficiency Test
French
German

**SAT II: Subject Tests (continued)**
Literature
Mathematics Level IC, IIC
Physics
Spanish
Writing

**Graduate Record Exams (GREs)**
Biology
Chemistry
Computer Science
Economics
Engineering
General
History
Literature in English
Mathematics
Physics
Political Science
Psychology
Sociology

**ACT** - American College Testing Assessment

**ASVAB** - Armed Services Vocational Aptitude Battery

**CBEST** - California Basic Educational Skills Test

**CDL** - Commercial Driver's License Exam

**CLAST** - College Level Academic Skills Test

**ELM** - Entry Level Mathematics

**ExCET** - Exam for Certification of Educators in Texas

**FE (EIT)** - Fundamentals of Engineering Exam

**FE Review** - Fundamentals of Engineering Review

**GED** - High School Equivalency Diploma Exam (US & Canadian editions)

**GMAT** - Graduate Management Admission Test

**LSAT** - Law School Admission Test

**MAT** - Miller Analogies Test

**MCAT** - Medical College Admission Test

**MSAT** - Multiple Subjects Assessment for Teachers

**NJ HSPT-** New Jersey High School Proficiency Test

**PPST** - Pre-Professional Skills Tests

**PRAXIS II/NTE** - Core Battery

**PSAT** - Preliminary Scholastic Assessment Test

**SAT I** - Reasoning Test

**SAT I** - Quick Study & Review

**TASP** - Texas Academic Skills Program

**TOEFL** - Test of English as a Foreign Language

**TOEIC** - Test of English for International Communication

---

**RESEARCH & EDUCATION ASSOCIATION**
61 Ethel Road W. • Piscataway, New Jersey 08854
Phone: (732) 819-8880

### Please send me more information about your Test Prep books

Name _____

Address _____

City _____ State _____ Zip _____

# "The ESSENTIALS" of Math & Science

Each book in the ESSENTIALS series offers all essential information of the field it covers. It summarizes what every textbook in the particular field must include, and is designed to help students in preparing for exams and doing homework. The ESSENTIALS are excellent supplements to any class text.

The ESSENTIALS are complete and concise with quick access to needed information. They serve as a handy reference source at all times. The ESSENTIALS are prepared with REA's customary concern for high professional quality and student needs.

## Available in the following titles:

Advanced Calculus I & II
Algebra & Trigonometry I & II
Anatomy & Physiology
Anthropology
Astronomy
Automatic Control Systems / Robotics I & II
Biology I & II
Boolean Algebra
Calculus I, II, & III
Chemistry
Complex Variables I & II
Computer Science I & II
Data Structures I & II
Differential Equations I & II
Electric Circuits I & II
Electromagnetics I & II

Electronics I & II
Electronic Communications I & II
Finite & Discrete Math
Fluid Mechanics / Dynamics I & II
Fourier Analysis
Geometry I & II
Group Theory I & II
Heat Transfer I & II
LaPlace Transforms
Linear Algebra
Math for Engineers I & II
Mechanics I, II, & III
Microbiology
Modern Algebra
Molecular Structures of Life

Numerical Analysis I & II
Organic Chemistry I & II
Physical Chemistry I & II
Physics I & II
Pre-Calculus
Probability
Psychology I & II
Real Variables
Set Theory
Sociology
Statistics I & II
Strength of Materials & Mechanics of Solids I & II
Thermodynamics I & II
Topology
Transport Phenomena I & II
Vector Analysis

*If you would like more information about any of these books,*
*complete the coupon below and return it to us or visit your local bookstore.*

---

RESEARCH & EDUCATION ASSOCIATION
61 Ethel Road W. • Piscataway, New Jersey 08854
Phone: (732) 819-8880

**Please send me more information about your Math & Science Essentials books**

Name _____

Address _____

City _____ State _____ Zip _____